Boys Before Business

The Single Girl's Guide to Having It All

Jennifer S. Wilkov &
Kimberly A. Mylls

New York

Boys Before Business™
The Single Girl's Guide To Having It All

Additional copies of this book may be purchased at a discount for educational, business, or sales promotional use by contacting the publisher through info@BoysBeforeBusiness.com. Visit www.BoysBeforeBusiness.com

Cover Design by: Rachel Lopez
Rachel@r2cdesign

ISBN 978-1-60037-707-5

Library of Congress Control Number: 2009937426

MORGAN · JAMES
THE ENTREPRENEURIAL PUBLISHER

Morgan James Publishing
1225 Franklin Ave., STE 325
Garden City, NY 11530-1693
Toll Free 800-485-4943
www.MorganJamesPublishing.com

In an effort to support local communities, raise awareness and funds, Morgan James Publishing donates one percent of all book sales for the life of each book to Habitat for Humanity. Get involved today, visit **www.HelpHabitatForHumanity.org**.

Dedication

From Jennifer:

To all the men with whom I have built relationships with in my life: Their contributions to my understanding of relationships between men and women, and most of all – myself in them -- have been true gifts.

To our readers: Celebrate the relationships you've had and know that you deserve the best of everything in your life. You really can and will have it all.

I'm pleased to share the path with you that works when you focus on your boy before business. I'm confident you will find and embrace your Prince Charming.

I'm delighted for you.

For David, the man of my dreams: I appreciate you and am so happy to have found you. Thank you for living the "having it all" life with me every day.

From Kimberly:

This book is dedicated to all the women who question whether or not Prince Charming really exists and those who wonder if you really can have it all.

The right man is worth waiting for. You deserve to have a great relationship and a great career… you deserve to have it all.

And to my Prince Charming, Rob, thank you for believing in me and for your constant love and support. My life is better with you in it.

I love you more each day.

BBB Philosophy

You can have a great life…
and you can have a great love…
when you decide what you want and
you put your relationship first.

We're going to show you how to:

Decide what you want
Find and sustain the relationship of your dreams
Live the life you love

Contents

Introduction

These days, much is written about women having their career be the biggest part of their lives. Striving for excellence in the workplace seems to be the message of the day. We believe that striving for excellence in your most intimate relationship is the key to success that women seek in every area of their lives. For many women, this will be an innovative approach to getting what they want.

Putting a relationship first might seem controversial for some and some women may even question our support of the entire women's movement. For years we saw women focusing on their careers and working hard for equality in the workplace, which we do support. However, somewhere along the way, it seems that we put our careers first and relationships second. We noticed a lot of women were having difficulty living a life that was fulfilling in every aspect. Women were struggling to have a great relationship *and* a great career. Something always seemed to suffer and the quest for balance seemed impossible.

Our hope is when people read our book, they will know that we support and encourage women to have great relationships and careers. When you finish reading the book, you will understand how and why putting a relationship first changes everything in your life and leads you inevitably to having it all. We believe putting people and relationships first is the key to success in every aspect of your life. "Having it all" for us means you have the perfect balance of a relationship and career that you love.

When we adopted this concept of making a relationship our priority, our lives changed and, as crazy as it sounds, before we knew it we were living our best lives. It wasn't always easy to practice what we teach in this book. We made mistakes along the way and were even questioned about whether we were reading our own writing. We made adjustments by using the tools outlined in this book. We learned that by continuing to work on our relationships and prioritizing them in our lives, our relationship experiences kept getting better. We found the secret to having it all and we want every woman to live the life she imagined for herself. Prince Charming does exist and happily ever after can happen for you as it did for us.

KIM'S STORY:

I had just turned 40 and I couldn't believe I was still single. Still single and never been married. I had always thought I would be married by 28. I don't know why 28, but it sounded good. I kept wondering, how did I get to be 40 without a trip to the altar?

I was a great catch. I came from a good family, was successful, owned my own home—so why couldn't I find my soul mate? I was stuck on this for a long time. Why don't I have someone? By focusing on the negative, the "I don't have," I got more of the same: no one.

The thing was I thought I knew exactly what I wanted. I even had a list of all of the qualities I wanted in my future husband. Even though I had the list and thought I was clear, I don't think I ever believed having a list was going to make my future husband magically appear. But everyone kept saying I needed a list, so I wrote it and I went through the motions. As the months turned into years, I thought, a lot of good that list did me. I was trapped, constantly asking, where is he?

Along the way I left doors to bad relationships open, just in case. My high school boyfriend was in and out of my life into my early thirties. I knew I was never going to marry him and I knew that he wasn't the one for me to have the "have it all lifestyle." But he was fun and easy to be around. He was in my comfort zone. I didn't think keeping him in my life would hurt. But I now realize that by not closing that door shut, a new door was never going to open.

In between my high school boyfriend I had other relationships. One was long distance with a person who was just getting out of a marriage. He clearly wasn't ready for a relationship but I thought he would be soon. So I was patient, always letting him call the shots and letting the relationship be on his terms. It was up and down and a rollercoaster of emotions. But I hung on just in case.

Just in case is never a good place to be in. You not only get foggy about what you want but sometimes you forget what it is you really wanted in the first place. The waiting game should be for no one. But that was the game I was playing—and it wasn't working for me.

I was hearing contradictions from people who wanted to give me advice. First I heard: Once you stop looking, you will find him. Then it was: You have to go out looking for him (with your list in your purse), followed by: You will know when you find him. My thoughts about everyone's advice were always the same: I didn't believe in any of it. I kept thinking he didn't exist. I had everything else and the only thing that eluded me was the relationship of my dreams.

I kept questioning the notion of having it all. Was it really possible? In my heart of hearts I wasn't ready to give up on happily ever after. I knew deep down that I still believed there was still someone for everyone and that I too would find him.

I joined an expensive matching making service, went out on three dates and met a great guy. We had lots in common and started to have a great time together. Everything was moving in the right direction and I started to wonder, "Is he the one?" I think I was anxious to have this relationship be it. Two months later when he said it was time to move on, I was shocked. It was a week before my 40th birthday party and I thought, "Wow, I am back to square one." I had a pity party for myself for a couple of days and then realized that with each person I dated, I was getting closer to what I wanted.

I continued to question the notion of having it all. I was convinced that there was a way and I decided to focus on my dream of happily ever after. I knew something had to change. I started with my belief system. I revised my list, changed the format to a new process I learned called the Dear God Letter. Then I got serious. I made a vision board with pictures of weddings and happy couples. I read the letter and looked at the board daily. I visualized what it felt like to be in the type of committed relationship I wanted. I pictured what we would do together and how we would talk. I went to the jewelry store and tried on my ring. I acted as if I was already in a relationship. I acted for one week.

One week later my Prince Charming came into my life. That's right—I said one week. A week after I put the finishing touches on my Dear God Letter, I found him. I found him when I wasn't looking but I was clear about what I was looking for.

Three months later we were engaged and, nine months later, married. I put the relationship first and I used the tools in this book. Every day our relationship gets better. I know it's because I was clear about what I wanted and I continue to follow the principles outlined in this book.

I know some of you might be thinking that sounds too good to be true. That it is not possible for you. Well guess what, I actually had met him two years before. In fact, we had gone out with a group of friends and went to breakfast the next morning. I vaguely remembered meeting him when we met again (through the same friend). If we had just randomly passed on the street I am not sure I would have even looked twice at him as someone I might have known and met before.

When we met the first time I thought I knew exactly what I wanted but I was wrong because I missed him. I missed this extraordinary person who makes me laugh, who supports and encourages me, and who I can talk to about anything.

All this begs the question, how did I miss him? I thought I was ready two years earlier. I thought I knew what I wanted. But I was never crystal clear. I was paying attention to the wrong details.

When I focused on not only who I wanted to live the rest of my life with but how I wanted to live, that is what made the difference. I focused on what I wanted to do, where I wanted to go, what I wanted to talk about, and what my life would look like with the man of my dreams. I focused on day to day events to future travels and how we would build a life together.

Two years later when he walked back into my life I recognized right away that this was the person who matched my Dear God Letter. He was everything I wanted and more.

It is important to close all your doors, so new ones open. It is important to pay attention to what really matters. Who do you want to hold your hand through the bad times and celebrate the good times with? When you are with the right person, the sky's the limit. As my relationship flourished, my career opportunities grew too.

I wanted it all and now I have it all.

JENNIFER'S STORY:

I was 39 and coming through the worst adversity I had faced in my life. Optimistic as ever, I wondered, am I really ready for the relationship of my dreams under all these circumstances?

I was divorced with no children and had just changed careers to the publishing field as an author and book consultant. My life was moving in a direction that was completely different from what I knew and was comfortable with. I felt like I was losing everything that I was familiar with. However, this was also helping me to clarify my reason for being here and what purpose I could serve for others.

I had beaten a debilitating disease, lived through and left a dead marriage, and was so used to starting over and reinventing myself that there I was again, back at square one—in every way imaginable. Financially, spiritually, physically, and emotionally, with no relationship, I was starting over. Some friends left when the going got tough, and others loved and stood by me.

I wondered if I was really ready to become the person I wanted to be, and what kind of relationship I really wanted.

I had been going out on a lot of first dates for a couple of years after I got divorced through a dating service, Internet dating websites, and kind, well-meaning introductions from family and friends. Halfway through the conversation during lunch or dinner, I would realize that the man I was meeting was lonely or looking for a one night stand and couldn't tell me what the ideal woman looked like for him. How was I supposed to know if I was the one who matched him if he couldn't tell me who he was looking for?

As for me, I wasn't so clear either. I knew what I didn't want. I thought I knew what I did want. I wrote it up: My Ideal

Relationship, My Ideal Mate, The Mate From Hell (What I Don't Want), and finally, Who Do I Have to Become? Who was I supposed to be on my own as an individual and who did I want to be when I got into a relationship?

I was clear, but not specific enough. And that got me into the cycle of dating man after man.

I was a believer in the idea that if you ask the Universe for help you'll get it. I decided to begin cheering the Universe on and identifying the qualities in the men I was meeting that I liked. I would talk out loud to the Universe and say the things I liked about the men I would meet. At first, the Universe and I were miles apart. I had to really think about what was good about the man I just met. At the beginning, sometimes there was nothing but the fact that he knew how to write a good email. I found, though, that I would get closer and closer each time. I was now seeking the man I wanted instead of waiting for the Universe to deliver him. I was partnering with the Universe and contributing to the process, not just waiting around for the next person to show up.

The Universe provided men of all shapes and sizes, different careers, and varying levels of wealth and sophistication.

This "sorting out" process was helpful and did help me get clearer. Eventually, though, dating became more of a chore and drain on my time than something I was enjoying. This was not how I wanted to spend my time.

So, I decided to work and focus on me instead of looking for him. I figured if I did what came naturally to me, he would show up in the activities and places I liked to be.

I decided that I would practice being with me and feel what it would be like to share my space with someone else.

I discovered the Dear God Letter process, and once again considered: am I really ready to step up and be the person I want to be in the phenomenal relationship I know I want to experience? I had been practicing for it and thought about what needed to be different in my life to welcome him in.

It took me a month to sit down and write my Dear God Letter. At the top I wrote: "Life treats you the way you treat yourself." This was a guidepost for me so that every time I would see the letter, I would remember to ask myself how I was treating me and check in. I wrote the letter, but I didn't give God any information specifying when to bring my ideal man to me. I just wrote down the traits I wanted in my man and in the relationship I wanted to share with him.

For two months he didn't come. I decided to review my Dear God Letter with Kim, knowing that I wanted what she now had. We made some small but important changes. It was then that I discovered that I had left out the information that I was ready now and I wanted to meet him soon.

I thought about it for a while. How did I want him to come in? What kind of man was I asking for? Did he really exist? For two weeks I pondered these instructions. And then I took the plunge and put together the concise description of who I wanted to meet, how I wanted to meet him and what I wanted as the overall foundation of the relationship.

I made a commitment to myself that when he did arrive, I would embrace him fully with my heart, soul and spirit.

Once I finished my letter, within twenty-four hours I received an email from a great-looking man on Facebook—someone I had never seen before. We exchanged emails and then phone calls. We found that we had been in the same training programs with people we both knew but we had never met. On our first call we talked for ten hours and before I knew it, the clock said 4:00 a.m. He seemed to be everything I was looking for, except he lived three thousand miles away. But I wasn't going to let that stop me.

Just two weeks prior to reaching out to me, he said he had decided that he wanted to be in a long term relationship and had identified the qualities of the ideal woman for him. He shared these with me—and so much more—during our marathon phone call.

And so, we talked and emailed and text messaged until we met, one day shy of knowing each other for four weeks.

It was magical. Who I'd found was a man who appeared to match my letter and my life.

I leapt into his arms and felt that life was never going to be the same again for me. Whatever transpired next, my world had been changed forever. He appreciated me and I let him. I did exactly as I had committed: I embraced him with my heart, soul and spirit.

As it turned out, this relationship ended quickly, after just two months. It was a complete relationship that had revealed one of the best lessons I have learned: I had begun to compromise on my Dear God Letter. I wanted to believe that he was the right guy for me, even though I saw and heard the signs that in fact he was not in alignment with what I wanted. I realized that

that was not the way to find the man of my dreams. Learning this was a big gift from this relationship.

We stopped dating and parted ways with a good conversation. By focusing on cleanly ending the relationship, I felt I was now able to open my heart to the next man I met without hesitation or unresolved feelings from this previous relationship. Closing the door quickly allowed new doors to open faster.

And they did. Within a couple of weeks, I started to let the Universe know that I was again ready to meet the man of my dreams. I refocused on what I truly wanted.

Before I knew it, another would-be Prince Charming came into my life during a professional networking event. I focused my activities on being the best me I could be. I believed that no matter what was going on in my life, it was the right time to meet the man of my dreams. Unfortunately, the man I met wasn't everything I was looking for, either, although he claimed to be. He had many of my "Would Like" traits and not enough of my "Must Have" traits. He turned out to be a great lesson too, a critical one. He had bi-polar abusive tendencies and nearly wanted to kill me during the short time we were together, just two months. I escaped from this frightening relationship and couldn't figure out what I had put in my letter that had invited this in. I learned a lot more about me and got very clear about some important facets of the relationship I wanted to share and the man I wanted to be with.

I realized the letter worked. I was getting what I asked for, but I realized I was missing many traits. So I once again adjusted, edited and added to my Dear God Letter. I went back out again to look with enthusiasm for my Prince Charming with a lot more experience with what to look for before leaping.

Sure enough, just a couple of weeks later, I found the man of my dreams. Actually, he found me—on Facebook. I was facing the worst circumstances of my entire life, yet I was confident that now was the absolute right time to meet the love of my life. He was and has been an incredible gift from the Universe. Our core values and beliefs were nearly the same and the foundation for our relationship was solid to build on. We believed we could withstand anything. We finally got it right.

Sometimes we choose to talk ourselves out of whether we are ready for a relationship in our lives. We think maybe we need to lose weight, change our job, live somewhere else, or have different clothes. The truth is that it's always the right time to meet him. Talking yourself out of the relationship keeps you from having everything that you say you want.

What I do know is if you are serious about wanting any relationship, then you have to ask for it now regardless of any circumstances you have in your life. Don't wait to lose the weight, change your job, move to a new place, or anything else. Go for it now. Get clear about what you want and ask for it. Define what you want and take the actions to go get it. Hold back nothing. You have to take action and make it happen. When you find your Prince Charming, make your relationship a priority and you can start living the life you love.

STILL QUESTIONING IF PRINCE CHARMING REALLY EXISTS?

Prince Charming exists when you define who Prince Charming is for you. As women, we seek a man who will fulfill us and bring out the best in us. How he does this is as specific to you as what clothes look good on you. The relationship has to feel good. Prince Charming is out there, indeed. It's the faith and courage to seek him that brings each woman closer to the man of her dreams.

Then what stops us from seeing the man of our dreams when he's standing right in front of us?

The picture some of us have of the Prince Charming from our childhood is a gorgeous, perfect-looking man who sweeps us off our feet and does no wrong. What we realized is, this idea of Mr. Perfect is crazy. There is no perfect person. But there is a Prince Charming for everyone. He might not be in the package we originally thought, nor is he riding some white horse—but he is out there.

We realized that many women have a mental picture of what their Prince Charming looks like. This can become a stumbling block in just getting to the relationship in the first place. Oftentimes, we saw women get stuck with an idea that the perfect guy is the perfect height and has the perfect hair color. We found that by letting go of your original mental picture, the door swings wide open for Prince Charming to walk into your life as is.

We know this because for years we dated a lot of frogs, we were hung up on certain things, and we kept dating the same person expecting and wanting them to change.

Our goal is to show you how to find your Prince Charming, how to have the relationship you want, and how to be a Dream Team. In the process, you will also learn how the principles in this book transfer to every aspect of your life and you will find out how to have it all.

How to Use This Book

**THE "BOYS BEFORE BUSINESS" PHILOSOPHY
ALWAYS WORKS**

It is absolutely possible for you to meet the man of your dreams, have a wonderful relationship and enjoy a great career. We know the philosophy works because it worked for us and we've heard from other women that it worked for them.

It's up to you to apply the principles in this book to get what you say you want and have it all.

Everyone has a different definition of what "having it all" means. For us, "having it all" is the ultimate combination of having an amazing relationship with the man of your dreams while sustaining your great career. Both your relationship and your career grow with you.

The truth is having it all starts with you. We will prepare you to have it all and take you through each phase. We will even show you how to get clear about what you want. But ultimately it's you who will have to decide what you want.

We don't know what's right for you, only you do.

This book won't work if you're not ready to have it all. You have to know the type of relationship that you want and the kind of person that you want to be with. Think about it: how can you find him if you haven't clearly defined who you're looking for? If you don't know who you're looking for, you will inevitably be disappointed with the men you meet and the relationships you have. This also holds true for your career.

How can he "measure up" if you don't have a measuring stick? He wouldn't stand a chance.

This book is designed to get you ready and to help you fulfill your dream of being in a loving, romantic, supportive, healthy relationship.

Let us guide you.
Have faith.
Get clear and apply the philosophy.
It really works – when you practice the principles.

HOW THE BOOK IS STRUCTURED

We're really excited for you to finally have the relationship of your dreams and sustain the career that you've worked so hard for. We know how personally rewarding it is when you enjoy both.

The book is written in a step-by-step style and takes you, the reader, through a three part formula to "having it all."

Part 1 – Prepare to Find and Meet the Right Man

Let us set you up for success with the Right Man. We are going to help you get clear so you can meet the man of your dreams. Then when you meet him, you'll have a much more enriching relationship right from the start.

We are going to help you identify what's important in a mate by understanding your core values first. Then we'll take you through an exercise so you'll identify more clearly with the type of person you want to meet. Finally, we'll share places to find him and tips to making this so much easier.

Part 2 – Build and Grow Your Relationship

Once you've met him, it's essential that you work on your relationship. The best ones grow and evolve because you choose to build them a little bit each day. In this section, you'll learn tools to develop your great relationship and discover how to keep lust alive. You'll also understand how to make sure his actions and words are in alignment with what he says and what you want.

Part 3 – Having It All

Apply what you learn in your relationship to excel in the workplace. We will show you how to have balance so you can enjoy both your relationship and career.

Each of these three phases contains tips, tools and techniques to give you a reference point to know when you are ready to move on to the next phase.

HOW TO READ THIS BOOK

The book is written in 3 distinct sections. The first section is all about preparing to find him and meet him. In the last two, we discuss how to sustain and build a great relationship followed by how to balance it all with your great career. The sections work together but it is important to understand that each stage is different. In order to get to stage 2, you must first complete section 1.

You might choose to read the entire book at one time or you might find it more beneficial to read each section and work through them one at a time. If you read the entire book first, you can get excited to see what's in store for your future. It will also help you understand the Boys Before Business philosophy and the mindset.

The book is designed to be a guide. You must prepare yourself first before you meet him. Once you meet him, then you can learn more about building a great relationship.

As you are reading we recommend you underline, highlight and even make notes in the margin. One of the keys to your success is doing the exercises at the end of each chapter. Once you feel you have completed that portion of the book then you can move to the next section.

You may even discover that you are familiar with some of the suggestions we've made. You might also discover that you have never actually used these principles during your past relationships.

Remember the philosophy works if you work the philosophy.

When you do meet the right man, you may want to go back to the first couple of chapters and just check in to see if you are on track.

We believe it is really useful for you go through the book with someone you know who is also looking to have it all. Developing an accountability partner will accelerate your success. You'll be able to share your triumphs, progress and stories with her and hear how she is working with the principles in her life. It's a great way to find him without feeling alone.

YOU CAN'T HIRE SOMEONE ELSE TO HAVE YOUR RELATIONSHIP

In our busy professional lives, we can hire lots of help for our business, to clean our homes, to walk our pets, and to provide food for us to eat. The fact is, we can hire anybody to support us with almost every area of our lives.

When it comes to a relationship however, there's no one else to hire but you. A relationship only happens and grows when two or more people commit to spending time, energy and effort together.

Building a meaningful relationship with a man requires your attention and his. When you are willing to contribute this to the relationship, you will get what you asked for. When you don't, you won't.

WARNING

Finding Mr. Right does not happen overnight. Building a great relationship and a great career takes practice and commitment. Having it all is a constant journey.

As you read the book and plug into our Club BBB, you might find yourself with a renewed sense of hope. This is good. However you might also feel frustrated that it is not happening fast enough for you.

You may even feel frustrated that you haven't used this philosophy before and this may lead you to have moments where you think perhaps you wasted too much time with the wrong person. Conversely, you may also feel like you've used parts of the philosophy and they didn't work in your past relationships.

All of these feelings are normal. Take a deep breath and realize you are at the right place at the right time and you will meet Mr. Right.

Having it all takes time, effort, communication, perseverance and patience. If you apply everything in this book, you will be in the right place to meet the man of your dreams, you will have the tools to sustain a great relationship, and you will know how to balance a relationship and the career you want.

Chances are there are going to be some obstacles and roadblocks along the way. That too is OK. Every relationship is different and we can't predict how yours will develop and unfold.

Keep practicing the philosophy and don't give up. We know it works and we know Prince Charming is out there for you.

"It's Your Time to Have It All"

~ Jennifer S. Wilkov & Kimberly A. Mylls

HAVING IT ALL

W hat if we *really* could have it all? What if there really *is* a success formula for putting men and business together in your life?

One of the most fun parts of being a girl is being a girl who has it all. We're always addressing the area of our life that we feel is "missing in action." It's either our work that's unsatisfying or our desire to be with our ideal man that seems to tug at our perspective of the charmed life.

We make routines for ourselves that address how we work, how we take care of our health, our looks, clothing and image, and how we choose what we eat and how much we sleep.

This is the fun part of being a girl. As the famous character Linda Low in the great musical, "Flower Drum Song" says, "I enjoy being a girl," and why not? It's great to be a girl. And it's also great to be a girl in love.

So how do you go from being a great girl to being a great girl in love?

Men have the capacity to swoop into our lives, sweep us off our feet, and swap our attention away from our business and onto them. Whether your business is your own or if you're on the fast track to a great career, those "healthy" routines we work so diligently to create somehow get tossed by the wayside when "he" walks into our life.

But you can have it all. You can enjoy being a girl. You can enjoy being a girl in love and a girl who enjoys her career. With the Boys Before Business™ formula, you can have time to follow your passions in your career and in your love life.

THE FORMULA FOR SUCCESS

We want to share with you our three-part formula to having it all:

1. Define what is important to *you* as an individual first—before you find the boy.
2. Decide what you want in a relationship. Be specific and identify the experiences and relationship you want to have.
3. Get ready to build your I.D.E.A.L. relationship. Let go and put the relationship with the great man you meet first.

THE MOST IMPORTANT PERSON IS YOU

What's important to you comes from inside, and subsequently reflects on your experiences outside. When you think about what's in your life and what you want a whole lot more of, you can weed out what doesn't feel good and focus your energy and effort on building a world that you absolutely love and want to share with someone else.

Take time to discover your values. Then you can determine who Mr. Right is for you.

VALUES ARE VALUABLE

Before you start matching yourself up with Prince Charming, it's important to get clear about your core principles. Think about this: What do you value in the people in your life today? Why do they get your trust and attention? Why do you want to be close with them?

When you think about the man you want to be with, be ready to share this information with him. Take a look through the following list of values and choose which ones are most important to you. If something is missing, add your own value to the list.

❤ Peace	❤ Love
❤ Intelligence	❤ Wisdom
❤ Spirituality	❤ Achievement
❤ Vitality	❤ Security
❤ Wealth	❤ Pride
❤ Health	❤ Community
❤ Cooperation	❤ Creativity
❤ Freedom	❤ Honesty
❤ Innovation	❤ Integrity
❤ Self Respect	❤ Family
❤ Loyalty	❤ Learning
❤ Order	❤ Power
❤ Recognition	❤ Accomplishment
❤ Advancement	❤ Affection
❤ Environment	

Once you have your list, you are well on your way. When you meet him, you can show him your list of values and ask him to share his with you. Understanding what's most important to each of you in a relationship can provide a solid foundation on which to build the relationship you want with your man.

If your values are different from one another, then you may find out very quickly why you just aren't connecting the way you would like to. This might be a signal that you may want to keep looking and meeting other men.

It is important to honor each other during this process. Go for the goal of understanding each other and how your individual priorities mesh. Value him and share your values openly. You will find that, together, you can create an even stronger relationship when you invest the time to support what is of core importance to each of you in the relationship.

"DEAR GOD, PLEASE SEND HIM QUICKLY"

Getting clear about your values is a great start. The next part of the process takes a little more time and a broader focus.

Deep reflection about what is important for you in a relationship is helpful when preparing for him to come into your life.

Oftentimes, women focus on what he will be like, look like, do for a living, how much he'll have, what he'll buy us, where he'll take us, how great he is in bed, and more. Whew! What a tall order he has to live up to. Does he really have to have brown hair, blue eyes and be over 6 feet tall for you to date him?

Focus on the relationship you want to have with him and define it clearly. One of the best ways to do this is through the structure of what we call a "Dear God" letter. This letter provides three levels of importance for characteristics and feelings that result from the relationship you build with him, instead of defining him. It is a tool to help you focus on the specifics of what you desire in a relationship.

Start your letter by asking God (or whatever you believe in) for what you want and state clearly when you want it. Be specific. It is similar to ordering food in a restaurant. Do you want the burger with no mayo and everything else on the side? You tell the waiter exactly what you want and you expect your order will come out right. Be specific about telling God what makes your heart really sing in a relationship and remember to let God know when you want it.

Define your ideal relationship using the following categories:

- "Must Have" Traits
- "Would Like" Traits
- "Dream" Traits

After you have it written go back and read it a couple of times. Ask yourself how you feel as you read it. If you read it and get excited you are on the right track. If you have written anything that makes you have negative thoughts, go back and rewrite the sentence.

The stronger your feelings are, the easier it is to accelerate the process. Put your order in and expect to get it.

Using these traits as measuring sticks help you decide what's really important and who you want to spend your time with.

For example, if you meet a man who has no desire to raise children and raising children is a "must have" for you, then he is not the one you want to spend a lot of time with since he does not share this same "must have" interest with you.

Here is an example of a Dear God Letter to get you started:

Dear God,
Here is what I am looking for in a man, or something better.
Please send him soon.

"Must Have" Traits

- Available and ready for a committed relationship
- Wants a marriage that is a life-long commitment
- Is honest, intelligent and can laugh at himself
- Is loyal, dependable and confident
- Ambitious and has balance
- Good in a bad situation and is optimistic with a positive outlook
- Knows how to relax and have fun
- Is open to new experiences and opportunities
- Fearless and goes after his dreams
- Passionate and makes me feel desired
- Loves music
- Loves to travel
- Addiction free and smoke free
- Good listener and supportive; great communicator; will work through problems
- Good with finances
- Has vision and sets goals
- Reads and wants personal growth
- Enjoys being active and fit
- Has a personal relationship with God
- Has friendships and relationships
- Has strong family relationships or has resolved them in a healthy way
- Practices integrity

"Would Like" Traits

- Plays tennis and skis
- Likes going to the movies
- Cares about appearance
- Spiritual
- Appreciates the finer things
- Socially liberal
- Proactive, "does the right thing"
- Cultured and well-rounded
- Respects the planet and values the Earth
- Has a flexible schedule

"Dream" Traits

- Is a motivational speaker, coach or trainer
- Loves to cook
- Wants or has a Labrador Retriever

Read the letter to God daily and take a few moments to feel the emotions attached to describing the person you want. Then get ready for your day and expect the best. Set an intention to meet him and let the Universe conspire to help you.

You can go to www.DearGodLetter.com/BBB to get more information and support with writing and using your Dear God Letter.

With values in hand and a new sense of clarity about who you want, you are now ready to start your journey.

IS IT LOVE?

Now comes the fun part. You find him. You meet him. You come home and check your list. You call your best friend and tell her you have checked everything off your list and he's it.

You're so excited you can't wait until the next day. You get just a little ahead of yourself and start planning your future.

You happily tell your friends that you no longer have to go out on one bad date after another. After the first date, you find yourself planning your first year and thinking of all the possibilities. Be careful of falling into this trap. This is called the He's Perfect on Paper stage. Even if you checked everything off your list, you still want to slow down and enjoy the journey. Sometimes what's perfect on paper ends up being not so perfect in real life. You want to manage your expectations so you are not falling in love with what *could* be, but with what is *real*. The trick is managing your expectations and excitement and differentiating between what's fantasy and what's reality.

You can have it all—you just have to know what you want. We want you falling in love with him, not with just the possibility of him.

The key isn't to look for someone who you can live with. It's to *look for someone you can't live without.*

So how do you know you've found the ideal relationship?

DEFINING THE I.D.E.A.L. RELATIONSHIP

We're convinced that there is a new recipe for success that builds just that—success.

The secret? Boys Before Business™. It's a new approach to the age-old challenge of how to have it all that will lead you to the I.D.E.A.L. Relationship you've always wanted.

When we talk about the I.D.E.A.L. relationship, we are referring to a relationship that flows through five distinct stages.

It starts with the Introduction then moves to the Disruptions that result from the impact of building, sharing and crafting your life to include him. It then continues through the state of Elation and the joy of being in the right relationship—finally. Then the time will come to progress through the stages of Attraction, Attachment and Action. Finally you will graduate from Lust to Love and set up your relationship for the Long-term. Your efforts will lead to a relationship that works for both boys and business.

We are going to show you how to have the balance that you might not believe is possible, the relationship that makes you smile every day, and a career that makes you proud. We are going to give you the keys to success for finding the I.D.E.A.L. Relationship for you. We are going to teach you how to embrace your new relationship and how it can support you in all areas of your personal and professional life.

Everyone's I.D.E.A.L. man may be different, but most relationships go through the same stages. In each stage, there are things to look for. We're going to share tips to help you keep moving forward through each one. This is the power of the Boys Before Business™ formula for having it all.

We've found that men and relationships don't come with a manual. It's important for you to be clear about who you are, what you want, and what kind of relationship you want to share and enjoy. Communication and being a willing participant will make your relationship so much better and a whole lot more fun. Relationships require time and attention, just like growing things in your garden. Whatever you care, feed and water will grow. So don't worry about the manual – it doesn't exist. We want you to focus on the I.D.E.A.L. relationship so you laugh and have a good time moving through each stage of your relationship.

WHAT IS "BOYS BEFORE BUSINESS"?

The media tends to label the single girl with such terms as "workaholic" or "married to her career." We want the new label for the single girl to be "she has it all." It doesn't have to be one or the other. Success comes from making time for both a relationship and a career.

Many of us obsess about these two areas of our lives. So, we go on overload with our attention. We drown ourselves in our work and career until we meet him. Then we overload ourselves with our attention to him and find our minds on other things while at work. Somehow the behavior is the same: obsess and overload about the man and do the same with our business. This is not the recipe for success.

Many women find the workplace to be a great place to build self confidence. They often use work as a way to fill many of the needs that we want from a relationship. Through satisfying careers they often get so wrapped up in their jobs that they sometimes think a great career is enough. But then they go home to an empty house and wonder, "Is there more?" The answer is: yes.

We were each that single girl. We were single and had flourishing careers. We had fulfilling lives and were constantly busy but we couldn't shake the feeling that we wanted to share it with someone. We wanted someone to encourage us and support us and inspire us. We wanted that person to be our partner, our friend, and our lover. Once we both found the man of our dreams, we learned how important it was to make that relationship a priority.

When we experienced the true bliss of being in a relationship with someone who does support us, we realized that we were missing out—and we don't want anyone to miss out. Our conclusion was simple. If we want to be in a fulfilling relationship, we have to put the man first.

Yes, we did say put Boys Before Business™. You may be thinking: this is going against what women's lib fought so hard for. We are saying that by doing this, you will focus on the relationship first and your business will still flourish. Consider this: if you can create a loving environment for the man in your life, you can learn to cultivate this same environment for your employees, clients, vendors and customers.

Take another look at this perspective: when you have love and support from a great relationship, it translates to less stress at work. Can you remember a time when you were in a relationship and you and your boyfriend were in a fight? You probably went to work and got nothing accomplished because you were so upset. Being in a bad relationship affects your work just as being in a great relationship can work magic in your career.

This is the real recipe for success.

So, read on and enjoy being a girl who gets the boy, the business, and the life of her dreams!

TEST YOUR "BOYS BEFORE BUSINESS™" BELIEFS

To test your beliefs, answer the following questions:

1. Are you ready, willing and excited to have it all?

2. Can you picture yourself having a great relationship and enjoying the benefits of a rewarding career?

3. Are you ready to do what it takes to have it all?

If you've answered yes to all three questions, then read on.

I is for
Introduction

When we live alone, we often create an environment that serves us—and us alone. We fill up our lives at work, at play, at home and in between with family, friends, professional success and ambitions, and activities that make us feel good.

We spend a lot of time talking to our friends about how much we want to be in a relationship. We go through details about what we want and how we envision our soul mate. We have a vision of what he looks like. We picture Prince Charming down to the last detail of hair and eye color and body type. We talk about who is "our type" and we spend countless hours analyzing what worked and what didn't work from past relationships. We form composites of all our past boyfriends to make the perfect match.

We know what we want and what we don't want. We talk about how we want someone romantic, and then we say we want someone spontaneous, or we change our minds and say we want someone mysterious. Sometimes we want a guy who is ambitious and then we say not too ambitious because we don't want someone who is a workaholic. We know what we want even when we contradict ourselves. We want him to be serious but funny, we want him to plan a great vacation but we want him to be able to do something spur of the moment, we want him to be smart but not a know-it-all. The list of contradictions goes on and on as we talk about every detail.

The question of "Where is he?" is a constant topic of conversation. We constantly wonder where have all the good men gone. We say we want happily ever after and we talk about how we are ready for Mr. Right to walk through the door. But are we? Have we really taken a look at our lives to see if we have made room for Mr. Right? Or are we so busy being busy that if Mr. Right walked through the door we wouldn't even see him? And are we so set on the picture we have of what he should be that we rule him out before we even give him a chance?

For example, test to see if you might be missing a great opportunity. Read quickly through the following paragraph and count the number of b's that you see:

Boys Before Business™ is about bringing balance to your life and living absolutely your best life. Whether you are looking for your husband or just a boyfriend, we want to help you celebrate and embrace your inner beauty. We hope to contribute to your success in finding what you are looking for and building your belief that you can have it all.

What's your count? How many b's did you see?

There are actually sixteen b's in the paragraph above. If you didn't see them all, imagine how many men you might be missing. This is an example of potentially overlooking qualities in the men you're meeting.

Oftentimes, when we meet somebody for a date, our first thought is that he's not the one. Our next thought is how long do I have to stay on this date to be polite? If we had an open mind, listened closely, and stayed a little while longer, we might find that he does have something to offer that is of interest. Be careful of judging your date in the first five minutes. Practice the art of conversation and practice the art of being kind. This in turn will help you attract the right person in your life. Look for the b's.

PREPARATION

To help you focus on preparing yourself for the amazing relationship you want, think about yourself and your life right now. Ask yourself if there is room for a man in your life.

Start with your home. Is every closet jam-packed with more black shoes than you need? Are the bathrooms in your house filled with cosmetics and products from years ago? Think about this: If Mr. Right came to your house, would he feel comfortable? Or would he wonder if he fits in?

Does this sound familiar?

- Making your bed is not a priority.
- You are fine with leaving dishes unwashed in the sink.
- Instead of taking a shower, you pull your hair back into a ponytail.
- You shop for food without a list because, after all, you're only cooking for one—if you're cooking at all.
- Popcorn is a staple for dinner along with anything else that can be made in a microwave in six minutes or less.
- Clothes are bursting through your closets—some you haven't worn in years and others still have tags on them.

- ❤ Your medicine cabinet is filled to the max and overflowing with your make-me-clean-and-pretty aids.

So, let's ask this question again:

Is there **really** room for a man in your life?

It might be time to start cleaning up and clearing out your space to make room for him. Take inventory of what you have in your house. Walk into your home as if you were a stranger. What would you see? Is every nook and cranny filled?

Turn your home into a place that would feel welcoming to a man, a place where you could see the two of you together, a place where he could put some of his favorite things. We aren't saying make room for the stuffed deer but do make room for him to hang a shirt or two.

MAKING ROOM FOR HIM

How do you do this? Start by looking around your life and observe what you see. Decide if you truly have no space for him.

Specifically, pay attention to the closet, your eating and shopping habits, the way you keep your home, and even look at the space in the bathroom.

Start cleaning up the clutter in your life to make room for him.

The easiest way to get started is with your closet. Yes, believe it or not, this is really the best place to start. You see, the proverbial "cleaning your closet" activities—physically and mentally—help you to make room for the man coming in. In the case of your clothes, shoes and other accessories you keep in your closet, take an inventory and go through every piece of clothing you wear. If you haven't worn it in over a year, donate it to a charitable organization and get it out of your space. It doesn't matter if it has the tags on it or if it's those jeans you swear you're going to fit it again some day. Toss 'em out. Be sure to hit your dresser drawers, too.

Cleaning out the clutter in your closet provides space for him to come in to your life.

Next, look around your bathroom. Throw away all the items you are not using. Go through all the bottles, cosmetics, brushes, hair accessories, perfumes and other medical items and clear them out. The objective here is to determine what you are really using every day.

He needs to feel comfortable in your space. He's got to be able to see a place to put his toothbrush, razor and shaving cream when the time is right.

Now the "inner closets": What about hanging on to things that other men have given you in past relationships? Perfumes, jewelry, cards, and other gifts may be hanging around in your environment, reminding you of past relationships that are long over. We suggest that you remove these items from your environment and either throw them away or give them away. Every time you see these items, you think of the man who gave them to you. This takes away your attention, thoughts and presence from the new relationship that you want to build with your new man. When you clean your environment and take this stuff out, you make the space for him to walk into your life.

He will want you to focus on him, just like you will want him to focus on you.

Many of us think we don't need to make room in our homes for him because if we meet him then we will move in with him or we will buy a home together. We fantasize about building our dream home together and we sometimes don't think about making our own home a dream home now. Why are we waiting to have the life we want? Now is the time to have your home be congruent with your life. Instead of picturing your home without him, picture your home as the dream home with him. This isn't a forever thing. Your dream home can still be a reality but what if you have it now and he comes? Maybe, just maybe, he could move into your house. So spend some time thinking about whether your home is the place where the two of you could be happy.

"CLEARING THE CLUTTER" CHECKLIST

Imagine this: you are now him.

1. Walk into your home and look around. What do you see? Is there a place to hang his coat in the closet when he has arrived? Where would he put his keys if he drove to your place?

2. Look at all of your closets. Is there any room at all for him to hang anything? Take the time and focus your attention on clearing a space for him. Make room for him to hang his shirts and pants and clear a spot for his shoes.

3. Walk into your bedroom. Is the bed inviting, with clean sheets, pillows fluffed up high, the blanket and sheet folded over neatly at the top of the bed under the pillows?

4. Check your bathroom and medicine cabinet. Is there anything you would be embarrassed about if he peeked in and opened it? Where is he going to put his toothbrush when he spends the night?

5. Walk into your kitchen. Are there dishes in the sink waiting to be washed? Is there a clean glass available to offer him a drink? Is it clean and ready to cook a romantic meal together?

6. If you have a pet, is he or she well-groomed and cared for? Is the litter box clean for your cat?

7. What does your home smell like? Is it fresh and clean? Maybe with the scent of a candle you burned last night?

8. Walk into your living room. Is the couch clear of stuff, cushions fluffed up high, just waiting for you to sit down and cuddle with him for the night? Are your DVDs stacked neatly so you can easily pull out the one that you want to watch?

9. Finally, go outside to your car. Get in and take a look around. Is there room for him in your car? Think about it: can he actually fit in your car with you?

10. Do you have a home office? Is there space for both of you? What if you both end up working from home? Look at your office space and make the appropriate changes to welcome him into your work space.

Make sure you make room for Mr. Right, so that not only do you see him but he feels you want and have time for a relationship.

If what you see is not what you would want him to see, make a plan to clean it up and change your routines so these areas and items are clean and ready to receive the man you're bringing in.

Key: If you want to do it for him when he arrives, do it for you first. Make the environment clean and clear for you so that you are already practicing this for both of you when he arrives on the scene.

You don't have to be Martha Stewart and we aren't saying be June Cleaver, either.

What we are saying is, let your home reflect who you are and who you want to be in the relationship.

PRACTICE MAKES PERFECT

You're doing fabulously. We're cheering you on and now want to take you to the next stage: practice makes perfect.

One of the ways we know how to build our knowledge is with practice.

If we want to learn how to play the piano, we take lessons and then go home and practice our chords and notes. Each time we practice, we sound better and better.

Funny, when we begin thinking about introducing a man into our world, we forget the whole concept of practicing and want to go from the single, busy female to a woman in a deep, adoring, loving relationship with a man. The only challenge is that we haven't considered how our behaviors will change when we have someone else around in our environment and daily activities.

Begin to think about what life will be like when you are sharing your space with someone else. As simple as it sounds, use the golden rule as your guide: do unto others as you will have done to you.

So, if it would bother you to see his bed unmade every day, be sure to practice making yours so he will appreciate your attention to keeping the bedroom clean and fresh for both of you.

If you enjoy coming into a clean, fresh kitchen to cook, or want him to cook for you, keep your kitchen clear and dishes put away so that every time you walk in, it's in ready-to-cook condition.

These are a few suggestions for activities you may do around the house.

There are also other choices that you may decide to change, including the hours you commute, the hours you work, when you would leave your office, and how you would spend your nights. Maybe you would like to call him for a few minutes during the day. Practice taking a time out for a few minutes during your work day to daydream about what it feels like to call him and gush about what just happened to you at work, or what you just read in the paper this morning on the train. Maybe you'd want to tell him how you would laugh at the kooky things your parents do and how they have no clue about how to get the email you just sent them.

Practice, practice, practice. It's not about being perfect. It's about feeling the feeling of what it's like to share your life with someone else.

SETTING THE TABLE

Here is a simple exercise that can help you get ready to support and include the man you are introducing into your life. Be open to the idea of practicing what it feels like to be responsible for someone else in your space.

Every time you prepare something to eat at home in your own environment, set the table for two. We know this might seem crazy and a lot of extra effort; however, this simple exercise will help you visualize what it is like for the two of you to eat a quiet dinner at home together or when you're out for dinner, for the waiter to say, "Table for two?" instead of, "Just one?"

Is your table where you would eat together filled up with papers and mail that need to sorted through and read? Get it off there and make room for him. If he showed up tomorrow, where would he eat? Put out a traditional table setting with napkin, fork, knife and spoon along with a cup or glass for a drink at the chair next to yours.

Prepare a space to welcome him and for him to join you for your meal. Think about what it would be like to have the opportunity to share this meal with him, to talk at breakfast about the day ahead, to chat at lunchtime about what you read in your book that morning, or to catch up during dinner on what you learned and saw that day.

You may decide that turning the radio or television off during your meal makes it much easier to interact with him and enjoy the great meal prepared for this wonderful moment of sharing love and affection. Start doing this now. Turn off the noisemakers and turn on the loving environment you're looking forward to sharing with him. Use this time to practice visualizing your life with him.

When you practice this exercise, think about how happy and grateful you feel to be sharing this moment of abundance with him. At first, doing this exercise may feel lonely or awkward. Keep focusing on what the experience will be like.

Right now you live in a certain way, the way you eat, sleep and live your life.

Do you allow yourself the joy of celebrating the meals you eat? Do you pause for a moment before you eat to be thankful for the meal you are eating and the person you are sharing it with? Do you actually take the time to taste the deliciousness of what it is you're eating?

Think about being in the physical space with him. Perhaps you could sit in a different chair at the table so you could see what it might feel like to sit side by side or directly across from each other while you eat. Maybe you want to turn on some soft music in the background.

OUT YOU GO TO FIND HIM

Now that you have made room for him, the question still remains, "Where is he?" The thing we know for sure is, unlike Prince Charming, Mr. Right is probably not showing up at the door. Maybe you already looked at the postman and the UPS guy in your neighborhood and decided they are not the ones for you. Chances are those are the only two people who come to your door, so it's time to go out and open new doors.

Before you go out looking for Mr. Right, determine what you love to do for your own enjoyment. We found that when you focus on what you love and enjoy, you'll meet men in the places to which you would naturally go. You don't have to do something different just to meet him.

You will need to ask yourself the key question:

What do I enjoy and what do *I* like, or, what do I want to learn more about?

There is no perfect place to meet someone. The only way to meet someone is to focus on yourself and do what you love.

If you love to do yoga, schedule your yoga class for the time that works for you. Notice if there are any men in your class. If not, ask the instructor if there is another class that has more men in it. Re-arrange your schedule to attend an earlier or later class that includes more male students.

If you love to go to the gym and notice that when you go no one else is around, change your scheduled workout time so you have the opportunity to meet more people.

Maybe you want to travel to Spain or France. Take a Spanish or French class at a local continuing education program. You may just find a man who is also seeking a similar travel adventure.

Tell everyone you know that you are looking for a relationship. Ask them if they know any great, single men. Tell them what you are looking for and share what you wrote in your Dear God Letter. This will help the people you're talking with to understand who you want to meet and whether they know someone. Being specific triggers people to think of certain people.

For example, if you are looking for someone who has a passion for the outdoors, specify that so it makes it easier for people to think of someone specifically who matches what you're looking for.

When you start to look for him, keep reading your Dear God Letter to keep yourself clear about what you want in your partner. Remind yourself that you are looking for someone you can't live without. There is no need to settle—you can have it all.

ASKING OTHERS FOR INPUT

Another way to discover yourself and what you want is to ask others for their input.

Here's a great, easy, non-invasive way of doing this. Ask your family and friends the following questions and take time to listen to their answers:

1. When have I seemed happiest in the past six months?

2. What activity was I doing or talking about during that time?

3. Was there a moment where you thought if I could do that for the rest of my life, I'd be golden?

The answers you receive to the above questions are probably the activities you enjoy the most in your life. They may also represent the activities you want to share with a man.

Trusted third-party perspectives like this can be insightful.

You can also learn more about yourself and what's important to you through a book, audio program, seminar or workshop. As Socrates said, "Know thyself."

ACTION: ATTRACTION

When you begin to define who it is you want to meet, it's important to look around at what you have been attracting into your world. Think about the men you have chosen to date and the men who have been asking you out within the last six months. Perhaps you may not have been out on a date in a long time and are not sure who you have been attracting. That's okay, too.

Understanding and accepting that we attract people into our lives can be a real asset in your effort to have it all. To best do this, it's important for you to recognize a simple Universal law called The Law of Attraction.

The Law of Attraction is a natural phenomenon. What you think about guides your actions and activities. You can use the Law of Attraction to create the result of your thoughts. So, get familiar with what you have been thinking about and creating in past relationships.

ATTRACTING THE ONE YOU WANT

The Law of Attraction sometimes seems too good to be true. Can I really attract the person I want? The answer is: Yes, you absolutely can. Start with knowing what you want. This is what we referred to in the Dear God Letter process.

Oftentimes, we have a list of what we don't want, and for some reason we keep attracting what we don't want. That, too, is the Law of Attraction working; however, it is working in the opposite way you want.

The Law of Attraction is about four steps: asking for what you want, believing you will get it, taking action, and actively receiving it. It is one thing to write down what you want and another thing to really, truly believe you deserve it.

BELIEVING IS SEEING

Asking for what you want is the first step; this is rooted in your Dear God Letter. Believing that you will meet him is one of the big keys to your success.

VIVID VISION

Here is a brief exercise you can do as part of your use of the Law of Attraction. Write down a vivid description of the relationship you want to have and enjoy with your man. Provide details in every area of your life, including how you will celebrate your relationship on a daily basis—whether you are at home or on vacation—and how your relationship will support your working hours. Read through your vision when you are complete. Now sit for five minutes and breathe in the feelings you feel when you read about your relationship. Feel these feelings and the tingles they generate for you.

To get the best results, read this vision each day at the same time and enjoy these feelings to the fullest. You can read it in the morning when you wake up and make it a part of your routine, and you can add it to your bedtime preparation routine before you go to sleep at night. These are both ideal times to set your mind on the great relationship you are attracting.

Think about how many times you and your friends

VIVID VISION
(continued)

have talked about how all the good guys are married or how hard it is to find someone you like. Did you ever receive a positive outcome from these conversations or did you receive more of the same—guys who are married or difficulty finding someone you like? The Universe gives you what you ask for. Change your words, your beliefs and your actions and you will receive different results. If you commit to the "what"—the relationship that you want—the "how" will figure itself out. This is the Law of Attraction. Your job is to simply be clear about what it is you do want and then trust the Law of Attraction to figure out the rest.

Becoming familiar with what it feels like to be with your man now is how you begin to believe that it is possible.

Take a few minutes to imagine what it feels like to be with your man from the time you wake up until the time you go to sleep. Write down all the feelings and emotions you have, and be specific. Act as if you already have what you want. Describe what you want in detail. Choose your words thoughtfully, because the Universe doesn't comprehend or understand negatives. So if you say "I don't want someone who cheats," the Universe doesn't recognize the "don't" and you still might find yourself in the same relationship time after time. Instead, say what you *do* want: "I want someone who is loyal and believes in monogamy." If you find yourself with a lot of "don'ts," just write down the exact opposite. If you focus on what you want, you will get more of what you want.

VALUES: MEASURING UP

An important step to take in the attraction process is to understand your own core values and what your focus is in your own life before you invite someone else to join you. Studies have shown that when two people get involved in a relationship of any kind—romantic, friendship or business—the relationship will thrive longer when shared core values are present.

Review the list of your own core values from your work in Chapter 1. Understand that when you are looking for a partner, you want to find others who share your core values. Decide that when a person has core values that match yours, they will be a good match for you to create a meaningful relationship. When core values are not shared, they should become signs that the relationship needs to end. Be careful of compromising your core values. For example, if honesty is a core value for you, then when someone is not honest with you in a relationship, this becomes a deal-breaker for you. The commitment becomes compromised when the other person does not respect this value in the relationship. This then causes you to want to end the relationship as you may not feel respected or valued around this person.

When you meet each person, ask them about their core values and principles for living. Maybe they, too, have philosophies and beliefs in their life that they live by. These are important for you to get to know so you can find out if they resonate with yours. You can also better support and relate to someone else when you become familiar with how they approach the world.

LIKE-MINDED THINKING FEEDS MAGNETIC RELATIONSHIPS

Understanding how you think and operate in the world gives you the power to approach the dating scene and your relationship from a more centered and focused perspective. We teach and train others how to treat us in our lives. By informing your man who you are, what's important to you and how you approach the world, you will provide him with the tools and details for how to give you what you need to succeed. It all begins by defining your values and the relationship you want to have.

MAKING TIME

You now understand the importance of your values. You have written your Dear God Letter, and you have some ideas of where you'd like to meet him.

The next step is to schedule time in your calendar to go out and meet him. If you don't schedule time to go out and meet new people, the TiVo at home will always be calling your name. If it's in your calendar and you treat it like a business appointment, you will get better results.

ENJOY BEING A GIRL

Making the time to look great makes you feel great and sets you up to meet someone great. One thing you want to do is make sure you always give yourself time to get ready.

It might sound silly but this can make the difference between a night that starts stressed and ends okay, and a night that starts off great and ends better. So, plan ahead.

Planning ahead means if you have a date on a weeknight, schedule your last work appointment to give you plenty of time to get home and get ready. Your other option is to schedule your date at a later time so you know you won't have to rush to get home. The last thing you want is to be stuck in traffic and watch the time slip away thinking about how you aren't going to have enough time to change, freshen up and feel great about how you look. Decide to leave work at a specific time and make no exceptions. If something in the office unexpectedly occurs, be prepared to work on this situation within the time you have allocated to work. This way you can get home and leisurely get ready so that by the time you meet him you are relaxed and look great.

Stop working and start focusing on him with ample time to enjoy the process. Primping, putting on clothes, applying makeup and fixing your hair all take time. Feeling rushed while doing this makes these activities feel like chores instead of a fun way to start your date. Imagine the energy you feel when you see him, knowing you have spent quality time to look and feel your best for the time you will spend with him. This is what putting Boys Before Business™ feels like. You will jump for joy when you see the big smile on his face every time he sees you. Chances are your work will never give you this kind of tingling feeling from head to toe. It just doesn't happen the same way.

A great way to give yourself ample time is to plan ahead the night before. Decide what you're going to wear so when you get home you aren't trying on clothes like a mad woman. If you have deadlines at work, think about working late the night before or working through lunch. The more time you give yourself, the better. It's better to be waiting than to be rushing.

Know what clothes you like and what looks good on you. Identify a few favorite date outfits that make you feel fabulous. Count on them when you are pressed for time. Now you can relax knowing that you will look spectacular.

If you feel good about how you look, you will have confidence. We aren't saying you have to be the next top model. We are saying that looking good makes you feel good. It also shows him that you care and that you took the time and effort to want to look good for him and for yourself. It shows him that he is a priority. More important is the fact that you take this time for yourself to look and feel good.

Ask yourself, would you want him showing up in a t-shirt and shorts to go out to a nice dinner? Chances are you wouldn't. You might even think he doesn't respect or care about you if he didn't take the time to look good. If he showed up dressed for an evening out, you would feel that you are special and that this date is important to him.

Men are visual people. When you look and feel good, you carry yourself with confidence—and they love that.

Whenever you leave the house, you want to carry this confidence with you, so ask yourself, do you feel and look good? Even if you are going to the grocery store, check yourself in the mirror. Every place you go is an opportunity to meet someone. Pretend your perfect guy is in aisle 5—do you feel like you don't look good, so you turn and run to aisle 10? We aren't saying go out in high heels and full makeup, but go out feeling confident and comfortable. You don't know where he is but you can control how you feel about how you look. You only get one chance to make a first impression. Don't have the first impression be that you need a makeover. As shallow as that sounds, men are always looking, which means if they looked at you, would you be proud or embarrassed?

Go out with the intention to meet someone interesting who will add value to your life. Look for people's greatness. The man you meet might not be Mr. Right but he might know Mr. Right or he might be a great addition to your life in a capacity you never thought.

Think of every opportunity that you go out as an opportunity to meet someone who might be a great new friend, a great business associate, a great partner or even someone who knows a great partner for you.

Keep being the seeker.

3

D IS FOR DISRUPTION

Y ou look great, you feel great, your home looks terrific, your car is clean, you have written down your values, you have finished your Dear God Letter, and you know where you are going to go to meet him.

You are now ready to meet him. You go out, and suddenly… whammo! You meet him.

The stars have aligned. Next comes the balancing act. How do you enjoy all aspects of the relationship *and* keep your head on straight at work? The new relationship is always exciting as you spend hours talking to each other, making plans and getting to know each other. It becomes hard to focus on anything else when you are excited about the new relationship.

PRIMED, PREPPED AND PRIMPED

You come home from an evening of pure bliss, knowing you have found a man you would like to get to know better. You walk into your home, look around and confirm that it is ready to receive this new man.

The support routines you have set up for yourself seem to be perfect. It feels as though nothing could unravel these routines for you.

You exchanged phone numbers, and so the telephone fun begins.

RING! RING! DO YOU HAVE ALL NIGHT?

He calls you the next evening to talk for a few minutes. You look at the clock and it is 9:30 p.m. You are excited to talk to him and get to know him better. You are not thinking about anything else.

Time just flies as you chat the night away. Before you know it, it is 10:00 p.m. and you just got your second wind, so you keep talking. Then you look at the clock and realize it is 2:00 a.m. and you have a 7:00 a.m. meeting or conference call. Now you can't sleep because you are replaying in your head everything he said.

The next morning comes early. You are exhausted the next day after going to sleep so late, and your colleagues at work, your boss, and your customers want to know if you are okay. You think to yourself, how are you going to balance this relationship with the rest of your life? After all, it was just one phone call.

When you find you have had one of those nights when you stayed on the phone for much longer than you had planned, celebrate that you have such a wonderful person to talk with and be grateful that time went by so fast. This is a great sign that you are enjoying yourself—and him. Accept that you were being present with him, investing in the moment, and acknowledge the consequences of the tired feeling you may have the next day. Take 100% responsibility for your choice to stay up and stay on the phone with him.

HELPFUL HINTS:
LATE NIGHT PHONE ROMANCE

We know. We've been there, and we've had the early morning meeting after being up all night on the phone. Here are some quick tips to keep the fires burning up the lines while you heat up your romance late at night on the phone:

1. Embrace this time and enjoy it.

2. These first few conversations are exciting. You're excited to talk with him. He's psyched to talk with you. Keep your focus on the conversation. Avoid multi-tasking like looking at your computer, the television or a magazine. Talk with him and have fun!

3. If possible, ask him to call you at a time that works best for you so you can spend quality time with him on the phone and still get the rest your body needs.

4. If you're in a long-distance relationship where you're living in different time zones, discuss making it more convenient for him one night and more convenient for you the next. This will help you build a supportive relationship that takes your respective lifestyles and locations into consideration. This is a primary building block for a long-distance relationship.

FOBFO™ – FREAKING OUT BEFORE FINDING OUT

Your relationship is now in full swing. Everything is going great. His actions and his words all match. You've found a way to balance the relationship and work and you seem to have a great system down.

Then it happens. He says he's going to call and he doesn't. All of a sudden your mind starts racing. You start making up stories in your head and replaying your last conversation, wondering if you said something that made him upset. Questions pop into your head like shock waves. Does he still like you? Did he meet someone else? Is it over? And the questions keep coming.

Before you know it, you're in complete freak out mode. You have no idea why he hasn't called, but you've thought of every worst case scenario. The computer screen is a blur and your work comes to a halt. All you can focus on are the assumptions you're making. You call your best friend and tell her it's over. Then while you're on the phone with her, he beeps in. You're in such a tizzy you wonder if you should even click over.

You click over, he tells you that the reason he didn't call was his cell phone died and he had to go get a battery. Think about it: Before you talked to him, you had made up every possible story, only to find out you were wrong.

You FOBFO'd! FOBFO™ means Freaking Out Before Finding Out. FOBFO-ing is the art of making up stories and panicking before finding out the truth.

"YOU'LL NEVER GUESS WHAT HAPPENED…"

Chances are no matter what the story is in your head, it's just that, in your head. Before you freak out, find out the truth. Give him an opportunity to tell his side of the story. If his actions and words have matched until this point, trust him. Don't sabotage the relationship or go into fear factor mode and immediately put your defenses up. Don't let fear stop you from having a great relationship.

Always think of the best case scenario first instead of FOBFO-ing. Practice patience and realize life does sometimes happen. Things do suddenly come up that are sometimes, just sometimes, out of your control.

Better yet, if you're at work, use this time to have a laser focus on your current project. If you're not at work, channel your energy into being productive or do something that you know will take your mind off the worrying. Some people will write, read, listen to some music or go to the movies.

The key to stop FOBFO-ing is to get into action. Once you're in action, any negative self-talk and self-doubt will be replaced by confidence, productivity and progress.

Avoid over-analyzing and making up stories in your head. This can get you in real trouble and create the illusion of a lack of confidence in the relationship.

To stop FOBFO-ing and start enjoying your relationship, practice the art of communication and the art of asking. If you're wondering if you're on the same page, ask him. You might not like the answer, but at least you'll know and won't have to FOBFO. There is nothing worse than guessing, especially when nine out of ten times you'll guess wrong.

FORGET THE FOBFO AND FOCUS ON MAKING IT FABULOUS

Instead of FOBFO-ing and complaining to the wrong person, complain to the person who you're upset with. If you're upset that he's late and didn't call, tell him. Talk to him *before* you tell your best friend or your mother what he did. In other words, tell the person who can do something about it.

Complaining to the wrong person can start another whole slew of FOBFO-ing. The voices in your head start to wonder if he's late because he isn't excited to see you. You complain to your friend, yet she can't make him get there on time, either. However, if you tell him this is something that bothers you and you want him to work on it, you have now communicated with the right person. If you don't like the answer he gives you,

you might want to think about if this is a person with whom you want to be in a relationship.

TIPS TO TRIP THE LIGHT FANTASTIC

You can go from FOBFO to a fantastic relationship; however, it will take practice, perspective and patience. By using the tips below, you'll spend your time being productive and building a great relationship instead of freaking out and wondering if you're in a good relationship.

1. Find a reality check partner. There will be times when you won't be able to tame the voices in your head alone. Call on a friend and tell her or him you want to hear the truth. Let her know you're looking for an unbiased opinion and you want to know if you're creating a story in your head.

2. Men and women often define time differently. Decide what phrases such as talk with you later or see you in a little while really mean. Identify whether it means one hour, one day or one week. Just get clear so you both understand it.

3. If something doesn't go as planned, don't worry about why or what happened. Instead, wait until you hear from him and let him explain. Be a good listener.

4. Use past behaviors as a barometer. If this is the first time he's late, don't assume the worst. However, if this is typical behavior in the relationship, it may be time to tell him how this makes you feel and let him know what you prefer.

5. Communicate. Let him know your expectations. He can't read your mind. Make it easy for both of you by speaking up and clearly stating what you want.

THE CHATTERBOX IN YOUR HEAD

There are going to be times when he might not be available to talk or spend time with you when you want to. These are the times you may find a chorus of voices in your head and FOBFO-ing might rear its ugly head. You wonder if something is wrong. Did you do something in the past few days that didn't sit well with him? Is he falling out of the relationship? Is he unhappy with you?

All of a sudden you may feel like the volume in your head is so loud that you're not sure which voice to pay attention to first. It may feel like rapid fire questioning or an interrogation.

Take a deep breath. Let's look at what's happening here.

THE MONOLOGUE

Once these voices begin to dominate your attention, you might find yourself feeling the need to respond by setting up a dialogue in your head to talk it out. The one piece missing from this type of conversation is that you may be "talking" with him, but he's not there to listen to you. So, what do we tend to do? We choose to answer for him, and go through each version of the answers we anticipate he'll give so we can get the issue resolved. This makes us feel ready for whatever answer he might give.

The challenge this creates is that you're resolving a situation on your own instead of allowing him to participate. This means that you're using a monologue to make yourself feel better, and you're leaving him out of the equation.

So what happens when you finally catch up with him?

HIS SIDE OF THE STORY

You feel that you know the conversation you want to have with him and what you think he's going to say. Let's face it: you've heard it all in the monologue you've been practicing. You think you know his side of the story.

In reality, he hasn't had the opportunity to give you his real response to the question or situation. So, this conversation can become confusing for him.

AVOID THE MONOLOGUE

When these circumstances arise and you feel the voices getting louder in your head, remember this: you have no idea what's happening to him at that moment. You also have no idea what he's thinking.

We suggest that, as an important part of your Boys Before Business™ approach, you call him, text him, or email him and ask him what is happening. Allow him to participate in the conversation.

Resist the temptation to answer for him in order to get the situation resolved. It'll be much healthier for both of you if you can wait for him to talk it out with you.

You probably won't be able to read his thoughts and feelings about the situation, so give him the opportunity to express himself.

If he can't respond to you right away, be patient. We don't recommend sending him eight text messages in an hour. We also don't suggest waiting three days either. Do give him the opportunity to talk with you. If he's not engaging, be aware of it and simply ask when he'll be available to talk with you. Keep those FOBFO-ing voices in check to keep them from disrupting a great relationship.

FROM GOOD TO GREAT

When strange situations pop up and you're tempted to begin the inner monologue, take a few minutes to put your attention on what's so great about your relationship and what you're enjoying about yourself as a result. Whatever you focus on expands, so put your attention on the good things that are happening in the relationship and discover new ways to make your couples time great.

Here's a quick exercise to help you refocus your attention when these situations come up:

Take a piece of paper and write across the top of it: "What's Great About This Relationship? What Do I Love About Me in It?"

Ask yourself these two questions several times and write down your answers.

Read through each response. Take in the goodness of the relationship. Celebrate the joy you feel about yourself, about him and about being in a magnificent relationship.

Take time to congratulate yourself for all the lessons you're learning and the blessings that come as a result of how you choose your feelings and actions in each interaction with the relationship.

Going from good to great in a relationship is up to you. Be the person you want to be in the relationship, and you'll find that putting Boys Before Business™ is a snap.

SLUMBER PARTY? OR SLEEP...

Talking on the phone and seeing each other has helped to build your relationship from one date to the next. You've been working on communication. The relationship is going great. You've minimized the FOBFO-ing, and you're ready to take it to the next level. Now the invitation to the sleepover finally presents itself, and you accept. You're tempted to stay up all night even though you know you have an early morning meeting the next day. What will you do?

We like to refer to this as the "slumber party," just like when we were kids. We'd all get together at someone's house, throw down our sleeping bags or pull out the trundle bed, and before you knew it we'd be up all night chattering away, playing games or telling scary stories. The next day we'd be pooped when Mom came to pick us up and, sure enough, by that afternoon we'd be napping on the couch or at our desks in school.

So how is this different than the good old slumber party days? Not much. We get tempted to stay up all night, doing pretty much the same things (okay, maybe not the scary stories). And, sure enough, the next day we feel exactly like we did when we were fourteen—exhausted and half asleep. Except now we have bigger responsibilities than just showing up at math class half awake.

WHERE'S YOUR STUFF?

When your relationship turns into a permanent slumber party, it's time to transition these overnights into some new lifestyle routines. The key is planning and organizing your day and life to work together.

As your relationship builds and you spend more and more time together, the areas which disrupt your original life routines are indications where you and your man need to communicate and coordinate and sometimes compromise in order to build a new routine that supports both of you. There are times when you might find yourself happily spending the night at his house, only to wake up disorganized and disheveled. To avoid the morning or evening chaos, there are some key activities you can do to help you stay organized, be productive and continue enjoying your relationship. To have it all, you will need to speak up about these disruptions and practice having a plan.

A great plan will keep you sane. You don't have to be a master organizer to enjoy a productive work and personal life. What you do need is a simple checklist. You need a checklist of everything you need for work and a checklist for what you need personally. Take inventory. Before you leave your house and his house get your checklist out and make sure you aren't forgetting anything.

One of the easiest ways to accomplish this is to prepare an overnight bag that's ready to go. When the decision is made to have you spend the night at his place or to run off on a surprise long weekend, have this bag with your comfort items and toiletries prepared. This will make the idea more inviting and allow you to focus on the joyful prospects of time spent together instead of having to go through the stress of getting the right things together.

When it comes to your personal care items, buy duplicates. Make sure you have what you need to get ready anywhere. Buy duplicates of your must have items and keep them in a bag that is always packed. Have a couple of extra items in your purse. The idea is to have what you need so you're never stressed or panicked. This also gives you the opportunity to think about what you really need.

Ask him if he has a space for you to put your personal items when you arrive. Perhaps you want to hang up your clothes and even iron them in the morning. Do you blow your hair dry after you shower? Find out what he has that you can share so you can also keep your bag light and easy to whisk away with you.

He'll be delighted that you're able to respond so quickly to the situation, and making the decision to go will be much easier for you. This way, you can follow your heart. Then, when you move forward with it, your life is set up to support you so you can celebrate the joy that results from this great Boys Before Business™ strategy.

The secret to the Sleepover: Be prepared to forget something and give yourself permission to learn as you go. Enjoy the sleepover. If you forget something, don't panic or beat yourself up. Make adjustments and keep the basics with you so you're never missing anything you really need.

SIMPLE TIPS FOR THE SUCCESSFUL SLEEPOVER

Sleeping over is just as much fun as it used to be, and so much more. Preparation is the key. Use these easy tips to make your sleepover a huge success:

1. If possible, make a date to sleep over on a Friday or Saturday night. This way you've got all night to play and the next day to catch up on your sleep.

2. If you sleep over on a "school night," if you can, make an agreement about what time you'd like to go to sleep so you're both aware of it. This will help you support each other with the other areas of your life while you're growing and building your relationship. You may even want to call out a wind down time so you have a buffer or margin of error on your "going to sleep" time. Remember to set your alarm to get up.

3. If you do stay up all night and just can't function the next day, call in sick and take responsibility for your choice to stay up with him. Pointing fingers at him won't get you to the relationship you've been dreaming of. Be 100% responsible for your own actions. Laugh about it with him and agree to a different schedule for the next time you or he sleeps over.

4. Don't wake up the next morning and act like a crazy person rushing home to get ready or, worse, wake up and realize you forgot work clothes. Plan for the night and be prepared. Pack a bag that has all your necessities. Keep the bag packed at all times so you know you have everything. To get more information about the bag and everything you need, go to www.BoysBeforeBusiness.com. Get up a little earlier to give yourself extra time in the morning.

5. Be happy and grateful and think about how great it feels waking up in the arms of someone you love. When you feel tired, think about something special from the night before and you'll forget you're even tired. You won't even need caffeine. You'll just enjoy the big smile on your face.

FINDING THE BALANCE

Your relationship has blossomed. You love the slumber parties. Maybe you have even enjoyed a romantic weekend away. You now have a good sense of who he is. It is time to check in with your Dear God Letter and evaluate how you're enjoying the relationship and how it's serving you and your new man.

To have both the man and the life you want, you might have to set up some new routines. This is what you've asked for, so embrace the change. Start to picture how you want your work life and relationship life to work together. Pay attention to how you are spending your time so you'll be able to enjoy the life you want. Think about some new disciplines so you can maximize every opportunity.

Be willing to endure some short-term discomfort as an investment in your long-term dream relationship. Reevaluate and reprioritize what's important to you to get the life you want.

Refer to your Dear God Letter for guidance and to remind you about what you feel is important. It's sometimes hard to distinguish between your must have, would like, and dream traits.

Here are some examples of when you may want to rethink what the true balance is for you:

Example #1: Marriage verses longtime commitment. You may have pictured your wedding for as long as you can remember but your man doesn't feel getting married is in his future. He wants to be with you forever and believes in monogamy. He wants a committed relationship—he just doesn't need the marriage certificate. Now is the time to ask yourself if this is a deal breaker. Is being with him without the wedding ceremony going to be enough for you? Are you willing to give up the wedding and marriage to be with the man of your dreams? You make the call.

Example #2: What about children? Many women struggle with whether they want to have children and if the man they meet doesn't want them. This can be a big concern for women, especially if they have dreamed of having the experience of being a mom. Be clear about what is most important to you.

For some women, it will be a deal breaker if he doesn't want children. If this is true for you, then be respectful and let him know this upfront. This way, you can determine whether you and he want to invest more time in building the relationship.

If you decide that it's more important to be with the man you're falling for than to have children, make this decision about you, not him. You have to prioritize what life experience you want to have: building the relationship with him or choosing not to be with him and having the experience of raising children with someone else or on your own. Whatever you choose, select the option that you feel provides balance in your life.

Example #3: Living in different states. You met him. He's incredible. You're checking off all the qualities that match your Dear God Letter. The only foreseeable problem is he doesn't live in your state. Under "would like" traits on your Dear God Letter you wrote "lives in the same state." So now what? Do you say forget it or do you find a way? This might be one of those qualities that you are able to live with. If it's the right person, give up wanting to live in the same place and find a way to make it work. This is something that you can make work. You might have had a different picture in your head of where you were going to live and how things would work, logistically. You can find the balance with the right person.

These are some examples of situations to think about and discuss with him.

FROM HERE TO THERE: TIPS FOR THE LONG DISTANCE RELATIONSHIP

When you're in a long-distance relationship, you'll have to think about what you'll need to address to make the relationship sustainable. Even if you're one hour apart by car, you're in a long-distance relationship.

For example, who is going to commute to whom? What time are you going to get together and when does the other person need to go home so they can safely get there without falling asleep at the wheel?

If you're in different cities and states, who foots the bill for the plane ticket? How long will you stay? And what happens if you don't want to stay and want to go home early?

These are all part of a long-distance relationship. Is it possible to make this work? How will you determine what to do first and who will go where?

Here are some easy ways to clarify this confusing situation:

1. Decide who will commute to whom.

2. As the commuter, become a master planner. Use your car time to listen to books on tape or personal growth CD's. Do the same on the plane. Carve out this time to be for you.

3. Let the commuting person dictate the time to get together and when he or she will need to leave to get home safely. Plan your date around their schedule.

4. If you're flying to another city, find out how much the ticket costs or how many frequent flyer miles are required. Agree to either split it, alternate visits to each other, or come to an agreement that works best for both of you.

This last tip creates a mutual investment in the relationship. This will also provide a great foundation for a discussion about managing joint finances in the future.

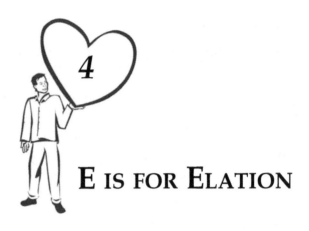

E IS FOR ELATION

It's your time to celebrate! You've met him and started to build the I.D.E.A.L. relationship with him. Now it's time to make more room for him and prioritize your time with him in your life. This is an important period where routines and habits in your life will be shifting, so pay close attention to what means the most to you. Open your lines of communication and keep letting him know what feels good for you.

Putting him first—Boys Before Business™—will help build a strong successful relationship and at the same time it will help you in all areas of your life. He'll feel you are committed to the relationship, and having a healthy relationship translates to a healthy life.

HE'S IMPORTANT

It's amazing how crowded and busy our days get. Sometimes it feels as though the very things we wanted to get done and accomplished fall by the wayside as we go through the unexpected events of the day. Putting your relationship with him first while focusing on what you want and who you want to be in the relationship is essential to winning the relationship of your dreams.

Get clear about what makes you happy and why you enjoy the relationship with him. Then, no matter what happens during your day, make connecting with him in the morning and at night a priority in your life. Set time aside to be with him—for example, at breakfast to review your schedules, at noon for lunch, or at night to just be.

When you're apart, stay connected by sending each other emails, teasing texts and loving messages throughout the day. You never know how much a great message can mean when he receives it at just the right moment in his day and he thinks, "Wow! I needed that!"

If you are traveling, make it a point to speak with him at a minimum at the beginning of your day and again at the end of your day. If you're in different time zones, make appropriate arrangements and agreements with him in advance to talk at times that work for both of you.

Men want to feel important and needed, just like women, so make him a priority. If you know where he fits into your schedule you can adjust your work schedule to enjoy your time with him. Make your calendar your new best friend and you'll be rewarded with a best friend in your man.

MAKE EACH DATE COUNT

When you're home, make a habit of continuing to date. Each week, pick an evening to spend together, like the way you would on vacation. Wear your favorite outfit. Hold hands while you walk together. Turn off your electronic equipment; it doesn't fit here.

Dedicate time for yourself to attend to the other areas of your life. Perhaps one night a week you have a girls' night out a night out alone. Schedule separate time for your romantic relationship with him. There will always be distractions. There will be times when you are together and other times when you're not. Be sure to enjoy the time apart and celebrate the time you spend together. You've prepared and cultivated yourself in order for this relationship to manifest in your life. Be grateful that he's here and treat him and yourself with respect.

Make a commitment and a plan with each other. Always commit to spending time with each other to build your magnificent relationship. If you did this just once a week, that would be fifty-two extra focused times a year to continue to grow your relationship. Make Date Nights a ritual and schedule them in your calendar. Be on time or early and look your best.

Become an expert about him. Listen closely and acknowledge him. This is the best form for dating that is consistent with the Boys Before Business™ philosophy. Oftentimes, just like you, he needs to be heard and recognized. Give him your full attention. You have scheduled this time to be with him. Everything else can wait. The dog can wait, your phone call can be pushed back a few minutes, and your email can be looked at later. Look at him. Listen to him with full eye contact. Open your heart and enjoy the conversation with him. Ask him to do this for you, too, so you feel important, significant and confident, as well. In fact, you will both feel loved.

Our goal for you is a happy, healthy relationship where the relationship with your man comes second in your life, after you. Be aware of your partner. Be considerate of him. Be willing to spend the extra time, energy and effort to make your relationship spectacular. We feel you will find it's definitely worth it.

While scheduling does support growth in a relationship, sometimes you may need to make adjustments. Be flexible. Leave room for spontaneity and surprises. Make the relationship count and have fun, no matter where you are.

ALOHA, HAWAII – TASTY TIPS FOR THAT ROMANTIC VACATION

When you go on vacation together, recognize that this is not every day life. It's a vacation—enjoy it. This is a different environment in which to get to know your new man. Steer clear of starting up routines that may not work in your daily lifestyles.

Be aware that vacations are excellent for getting to know each other better. Use this time to celebrate each other.

A few Boys Before Business™ suggestions for vacations:

1. Limit the disruptions to your time with him. Let your boss and colleagues know that you are on vacation.

2. Turn off your Blackberry.

3. Turn off your cell phone.

4. Leave your laptop at home.

5. If you're going to work at all on your vacation, make your man aware of your intentions and come to an agreement about when you'll be working. This will help him to be more supportive during these times.

6. Plan something special for him for the beginning, middle and end of the trip.

Fun suggestions might include:

1. Bring something with you that you know you can enjoy together while you're on the plane, such as a game or a movie.

2. Find a great card to give to him when you first arrive at your destination.

3. Bring a camera to capture your great vacation moments. At the end of the trip—and possibly when you return home—provide him with a snapshot from your trip accompanied by a thank you note letting him know what a wonderful time you had. This acknowledges all the effort he may have gone to in order for you both to enjoy a spectacular experience together.

Before you know it, you'll be planning trips together more frequently because it will feel like this is your time to spend with each other without friends, family, work or interruptions—just you and him, alone together at last.

ACTIONS SPEAK LOUDER THAN WORDS

Your priorities are in order. You're still celebrating your relationship, and everything is perfect…or is it? Be careful of falling into the trap of wanting a relationship so much that you don't pay attention to the details. The details you want to focus on are whether his actions and words coincide with each other.

Is he telling you how much he wants to see you but he never makes plans? Is he making plans but never following through? The old adage, "Actions speak louder than words," definitely holds true when it comes to relationships. We want you to enjoy both his actions and his words.

Many times, we find ourselves making excuses for our man. We say, "Oh he's really busy at work." Or we say that something came up with his family. There are a million excuses that we justify because we want to believe he is "the one" or we think he has great potential. We don't want to fall in love with potential. We want to fall in love with who he is today.

Enjoy your relationship and pay attention. Is what he's saying matching up with what he's doing? Do you know how he really feels about relationships? Did you listen to what he said? And, more importantly, are you getting the relationship you want?

If his actions and words match, you're more likely to have a stress-free relationship, which can help support a stress-free work environment. If his actions and his words are different, then you start to spend your time analyzing and FOBFO-ing. These two activities cause disruption in your work and life.

Understand that relationships will involve both highs and lows, so cultivate your relationship. Great relationships have great communication. If you find you're spending your time in a relationship that you are constantly questioning or find yourself making up excuses, this is the time to re-evaluate this relationship. This can be all-consuming. You're likely to lose focus on all other aspects of your life, and this can cause chaos at work.

We often hear things like, "Leave your personal life at home," or "Just focus on work." Although these concepts are great in theory, they are not realistic. If you're stressed in a relationship, it'll carry over to your work. You won't be able to think as clearly as you want. The same bodes true if you're frustrated at work. Work can carry over to your personal relationship. Being unhappy at home or at work affects the other environment, whether we like it or not. Using the Boys Before Business™ philosophy, put your relationship first. A happy home life will make it easier to have a happy, healthy work life. Cultivate happiness in your relationships at work and at home and everyone will notice how happy you are.

Know that you're going to need time, effort and imagination to make a great relationship. It will also be important to trust your intuition. If you're questioning his actions and his words, it's time to ask him questions. You might feel uncomfortable confronting him if this is a new relationship. However, you can't avoid a situation or how you feel, you can only delay those emotions and outcomes. Avoiding confrontation will hold you back from success in all aspects of your life.

You deserve to have someone who does what he says he's going to do. If those voices in your head have questions, don't make excuses. Listen to your inner voice. Instead of asking yourself questions, ask him.

Most people are afraid to ask important questions because they are afraid of the answers. Asking is the only way to stop wondering so you can move forward with the relationship and life you want.

HAPPINESS IS CONTAGIOUS

When you use the Boys Before Business™ philosophy, you may find that this results in greater productivity and happiness in your business and life. The happiness you feel may be radiating from you as you swing through the doors of your office or place of business. Colleagues may ask you what is new in your life and comment on the glow you have from head to toe.

Celebrate the love you share. It'll shine through to your working life, too. The happiness you feel is contagious. Clients and business colleagues will recognize this in you and, in some cases, you may inspire your co-workers with your relationship.

Oftentimes, you won't have to say a word. The way you carry yourself, the clothes you wear, and the way you communicate without words say much more about you than what you might say verbally. When you are in a happy, healthy relationship, you naturally feel great and dress well. It shows.

You may also find yourself smiling all the time. You think about your present and future with him and feel your heart skip a beat. You find yourself up late at night and early to rise because you're so excited to start and end the day with him.

This is the time to excel at work. This is the time to use your excitement to motivate your team, find new customers, pitch that great idea, take on a new project, complete a project and even ask for a raise. This is the time to talk to everyone.

Your excitement will be contagious and people want to follow those who sound passionate. The fact is, people pay more attention to how you say something rather than what you're saying—so say something. People typically only hear 7% of what you say. 93% of what they hear is how you're saying it.

When you are happy in one area of your life, it's easy to transfer those emotions to the other areas of your life. Have you ever been with your work colleagues and one person starts talking about how they hate their job? They start talking about everything that's wrong with the company. Before you know it, everyone is chiming in with what they don't like. The negativity becomes contagious.

The same is true for being positive. If you're positive about your relationship, it's easier to be positive at work. Make your positive attitude the one that sticks.

CELEBRATE GOOD TIMES

You've worked hard to get ready for him to join you in your life. Now, he's here. Cheer yourself and him, and share this wonderful enthusiasm through your work. Your commitment and efforts begin to pay off as you see results in your business and relationship.

The Boys Before Business™ philosophy leaves you with a wonderful feeling that you can take everywhere you go. Take it to work and see what happens in your business. Take it to your other relationships with family and friends. Life is richer when you feel this way all the time. Start enjoying it now.

Hey! You're glowing!

TIPS FOR TRANSFERRING
THE BOYS BEFORE BUSINESS™
PHILOSOPHY TO YOUR LIFE

Schedule time with the other people in your life who are family and friends. You now know some simple ways to make them feel important too and know that you care about them. Here are some quick and easy ways to transfer the Boys Before BusinessTM Philosophy to these relationships:

1. Make sure when you are spending time with your family, friends, co-workers, colleagues and clients, you are 100 percent present and use the same listening skills you use with your man with them.

2. Just like in your romantic relationship, stop FOBFO-ing and making up stories in your head about these relationships. Avoid the monologue and allow each person to tell you what they think, what happened if something doesn't go right, and how they really feel about a situation or you.

3. You know how your man likes to get a text, an email and a voicemail message, or a note from you – so do other people. Send a client a note of appreciation. Call your mom for no reason. Text a friend about how glad you are to be friends. Do the same things you do to make your man feel important for everyone else in your life.

4. Honor your commitments. Just as you would leave work on time to meet your man, show up for everyone else on time. If something unexpected comes up and you need to cancel, contact them as soon as possible to let them know and to reschedule.

5. Just like in your relationship, be flexible, allow for spontaneity, and enjoy the other relationships you have too. This is truly what having it all feels like.

5

A IS FOR ATTRACTION, ATTACHMENT AND ACTION

Enjoy the relationship you have and keep the attraction going. Learn to let go and work with your man to define commitments that give time and attention to both of you—for yourselves as individuals, each other as partners, and to your career fulfillment. Communicate openly and tell the truth about how you feel when you are together and how you feel when you are apart. Be a dynamic team. You can move mountains together and grow forward as a loving couple.

"I'M SO INTO HIM"

As you celebrate the relationship you finally have, you may begin to feel your focus is shifting. Where your work used to be your main focus, now suddenly your main focus is your relationship. As a result, you may need to make changes in your schedule at work to make room for your relationship.

If you begin to feel as though your work is interrupting your relationship, take time to reevaluate. Acknowledge that this type of attraction and attachment can engulf you in an unproductive approach to the relationship. It can become suffocating to your mate and may preclude you both from growing as individuals. We want him to be your priority, but we don't want him to be your only priority.

The I.D.E.A.L. relationship supports both people to accept, acknowledge and love who they are today and who they want to become. This happens through the natural ebb and flow of the day-to-day relationship interactions. Trusting each other and supporting the dreams of the other help to provide positive energy and create a healthy relationship.

It's like feeding and watering a plant. If you give it too much food, water or sunlight, it will die. If you pay just enough attention and engage fully in the moments with your partner, you'll find that you have more freedom in the relationship to grow and connect. If you overwhelm the other person with your attachments to them and make your happiness and self-esteem dependent upon the relationship, you may find that your partner will become uncomfortable with you because he wants you to be self-sustaining as an individual.

In the I.D.E.A.L. relationship, you both are there because you choose to be. It is a self-sustaining model for both an individual and a couple. Be both.

LET IT BE

When the relationship is free to grow and expand through your natural activities with your man, everything begins to blossom. Your self-esteem will jump up as you feel the freedom of being yourself in the relationship and speaking up for what you want and need.

Talk with your mate about the best ways you can keep your focus on your work and to grow individually. Let him become a part of the process instead of an interruption. Give him the opportunity to contribute to your success.

Start this process by making commitments with each other to support the relationship you want to have. These are the biggest focuses that will keep your love alive. These routines feed the desires and needs of each person without making either one of you dependent on the other.

Now start to think about what your partner can do to help you with your work. Celebrate your successes with him. Let him take you out to dinner so you can dress up and be the focus of attention. This gives him a stake in your success.

COLLABORATION IS THE KEY

Find other ways of identifying behaviors that nurture each other—both in the relationship and when you're working on other parts of your life. Share your goals, deadlines and project deadlines with each other. This is where you really start to collaborate.

Collaborating means taking the best of each person and asking your partner to lend their strengths to you. If your partner is a good listener, then talk things out with him. Let him become a sounding board so you can get it out. If you are more analytical and your partner is more creative, chat about a project to get his perspective.

When you start working together to support your goals and dreams, your relationship will grow exponentially and you'll both feel fulfilled and happy.

THE DREAM TEAM

We want it all, we want the fairy tale. Once we believe that we can have it all, we have to embrace the feeling and accept the greatness of what we have.

There's no need to sabotage. Recognize that this may be the first time ever that you've really gotten what you want, the fairy tale. No need to test it or chase it away. Instead, enjoy it and find new ways to embrace it. You'll find that the more you get into the relationship, the more it will get into you.

In order to have it all, you want your partner to be just that—a partner. Similar to your business or work environment, finding the right partner can make or break you. You will know you have found the right partner when you work as a team. We didn't really know what that meant. In fact, we didn't know *what* we didn't know. Here's what we know now: Working as a team means you communicate, make decisions together and, at times, compromise.

There might be times when you have to compromise on things you want in the short term in order to secure your long-term dream. For example, it is Sunday and he wants to go to the sports bar and you would rather go shopping. You have a decision to make. Are you going to put your relationship or shopping first? Do you want to spend time with him or time at the mall?

These small gestures can make all the difference for the man in your life. Show him he's more important by choosing to spend the time with him instead of shopping. As a result, there's a good chance that, when you want him to go shopping with you, he'll join you just as you did with him.

We aren't saying every Sunday you need to be at the sports bar with him, but make those choices that are going to build your relationship. Ask yourself what you would rather be doing and decide if in the short term this is going to benefit the relationship. Spend time thinking about the decisions you're making and whether they're going to help you with your long-term goal of having the I.D.E.A.L. relationship. If you want him to spend more time with you, then you need to be committed to spending more time with him. If you want him to be more affectionate then be more affectionate first. He's not a mind reader. Design the relationship you want by clearly communicating the things you want to share: time, activities, affections, celebrations, and more.

HINTS TO KNOW IF HE'S THE ONE

Here are some things to look for to affirm you are with the right partner for you:

1. You are your authentic self. You don't hold back. You're open and feel like yourself. You're not hiding anything. You freely share your thoughts, feelings and emotions.

2. You're attracted to him. You get excited when his number pops up on caller ID. When he reaches out to hold your hand, every cell in your body tingles with anticipation.

3. He's attracted to you. You feel it. You know it, and you never second guess. You're confident that his feelings are true.

4. The relationship is effortless. You are yourself. He is himself, and you can productively grow together.

5. You bring out the best in each other. His actions and words match, and so do yours. You support each other's goals and visions. You can't wait to talk or spend more time together.

If you answered yes to all of these, you know you are going in the right direction.

WITH ALL YOUR FAULTS, I LOVE YOU STILL

Think about how you feel about each activity. Use your Dear God Letter and keep in mind what you wrote. No one is perfect. Everyone has great qualities along with those qualities that need work. You don't want to trade in a great relationship because there are a few things that bother you, just to get a new relationship with an entirely different set of issues. Review your must have traits and remind yourself about what is a deal breaker for you.

Your short-term actions create great habits that lead to your long-term success. Everything you do on a daily basis is part of your relationship. You might need to get up earlier or stay up later in the short term to ensure your partner knows he's a priority. For example, if you're missing your morning workout and this is a priority for you, then decide how many mornings you're okay with missing it. Or, tell him this is important and why and collaborate to work out together, or determine how many workouts you're committing to in your schedule. These types of decisions are going to be critical to the quality and success of your relationship.

TIME FOR BALANCE

When it comes to managing your time, recognize that the activities you choose are what take up your time. Decide which activities are worth keeping in your schedule and which are worth giving up in the short term in order to spend more time with your man. Building a wonderful relationship also includes balance. To have balance, keep the routines that support you individually and add the ones that make a great couple.

STICK TO YOUR STRENGTHS

Recognize your strengths in your personal and professional life. Find out the strengths of your man and what he enjoys most. Ask for help in areas that aren't your strengths. For example, if cleaning your house is not one of your strengths and you find yourself spending hours on the weekend cleaning, this takes you away from him and gives you something to do that you don't enjoy. Hire someone to help you with this so you can free up hours of time to spend with him. Your house will be clean, you'll both enjoy being in it, and neither of you will have lifted a finger.

PEAK PERFORMANCE

Know your peak times of performance and happiness. If you know that you're a morning person, then make sure you spend the morning with your man. By understanding how you feel at different hours in the day, you'll be able to maximize your time at work and at play. Most of us have times in the day where we're more productive than at other times. Experiment and identify at what times you're best at work and what times are great for the relationship. Maybe you like to end your day talking to your man because that's the only time you feel you can be present. If this sounds familiar, make sure you always make a point to connect with him in the evening, if that is your peak time for happiness.

Find out his peak times of performance and happiness. When you both have high energy and interest, the relationship will seem effortless and grow quickly. If one of you is less engaged in the conversation or activity you're doing, it may be a bit confusing for you and may lead to a FOBFO™. Plan time together at least once a day where your peak times are the same.

What do you do when peak times don't match? This is where the Boys Before Business™ philosophy can help. Talk openly with your man about when you're in "prime time" for the relationship and when you feel happiest, strongest and most vibrant during your day. Ask him to share the same with you. Determine a way to alternate the times you come together in the relationship so you can realign your activities one day to be in peak state for his time, and ask him to do the same for you on the next day.

There is a Universal Law in nature that states, "You will become what you are around." We believe that if you work with your peak time and learn to align with his peak time, you'll train your body, mind and spirit to be in sync with each other's peak times. The more you interact at the designated time, the more you train yourself to be engaged with each other at that moment instead of demanding it at your own time.

Your body has its own clock and energy cycle. Learn how to work with this to support what you want to enjoy in your life. Fully engage in understanding your own body, mind and spirit, and understand what you need to reach a peak energy state. Then work through your day and arrange your activities, food, schedule and travel times so you can be at a peak state when it's time to focus on your relationship.

SETTING BOUNDARIES

Setting boundaries is one of the hardest things to do. We often have a hard time saying no to people. We want to make other people happy and we want everyone to like us. Setting boundaries is about making you happy first. By setting boundaries, you can go from feeling rushed, frazzled and exhausted to calm, cool and collected.

Start with small concepts, such as turning your phone off at 7:00 p.m. for your dinner hour, or getting into bed with the lights out by 11:00 p.m. Practice saying no to things you don't want to do and say no to things that don't challenge you.

Let the people close to you know that you have set boundaries and let them know what they are so you can get support from your family, friends and co-workers. Be clear about what boundaries you are setting and why. See what works and what might need to be adjusted.

TIPS FOR TALKING CLEARLY

Practice clear communication with the people you spend the most time with to set you up for success. Communicating your boundaries with your man, family, friends and colleagues will best position you to ask for what you want and get great results.

Clarity comes from understanding that you are asking for what you want. This is different than saying what you "need." Need indicates that you are looking for something outside yourself. In Boys Before Business™, we believe that everything you need is within you. When we ask others for support, we tell them what we "want" so they can assist us with insight and enthusiasm.

Some ways to ask to get the support you want may sound like this:

"I'd really like your support and input. I want to have more balance in my life, and I'm developing a new schedule."

"I want your support as I make some changes in my daily routine."

"I'm really excited about my new relationship. I'm balancing my work and personal life. I'm asking you to be patient and supportive as I embrace my new relationship."

There will be times when you might fall short of keeping your boundaries. This is okay, as this is an evolving process. You may need to make adjustments along the way. Keep clarifying your boundaries. It'll become easier to say no to friends and family while sustaining great relationships with everyone.

Working as a team, you can have the balance, quality, and success in your relationship. It's better together!

L Is For Love
Lessons For a
Lifetime

If you're still look for your Prince Charming, it's important to understand that people come into your life for reasons, seasons and lifetimes.

After each relationship, you'll want to evaluate what worked and what you'd like to see and do differently in your next relationship. Each relationship will get you closer to finding Mr. Right and building the type of relationship you want.

If your relationship lasts for a couple months and is just for a reason, look at the lessons learned and keep practicing the principles of defining what you want. Recognize that sometimes what you want changes along the way.

Love lessons last a lifetime, whether you find Prince Charming on your first date or many dates later. Love is a lifetime participatory sport. It is a life experience that grows with practice, attention, time and effort.

The Boys Before Business™ philosophy provides you with tools and techniques to integrate into your relationship efforts.

We're excited about what you're learning and the relationships ahead of you.

If you're reading along and find a great man, and then find that the relationship needs to end, we encourage you to complete the relationship cycle with him and then keep dating. Remain open to the love relationships ahead of you. Know that the man for you is out there and that the lessons you learn from each relationship are getting you closer to the man and relationship of your dreams.

Here's how to maximize each experience:

EVERY RELATIONSHIP COUNTS

Maybe you find that you're hopping from date to date or relationship to relationship. We are excited for you. You're allowing yourself to grow and practice what you're learning as you build your relationship skills and muscles.

Think about it: Have you ever started something that you were an immediate expert in? Most activities and skills that we have in our lives take time, energy, effort and our attention to make them stronger every day. We usually don't become an expert overnight, so we encourage you to stay open-minded and quickly end the dates or relationships that you find are not productive and in alignment with your Dear God Letter. Keep looking for the next man to date and focus your attention on the new man who is coming into your life.

Cheer yourself on as you continue to get clearer about who you want to be with and what you want to experience in your I.D.E.A.L. relationship.

If you don't find Prince Charming on the first date, it doesn't mean you aren't on the right track to find him. It means you're that much closer to meeting him.

CLARITY VS. COMPROMISE

Clarity comes through refining our ideas about the relationship we want to build. Sometimes, we feel strongly about a particular trait or experience, yet when we get it, our desire to have this may not be what we thought it would be. So, getting clear comes from opportunities to better understand what traits you feel are important in the relationship of your dreams.

Sometimes we get caught up in the excitement of the relationship itself and temporarily lose sight of what's really important to us in a sustainable relationship. Be aware of compromising your must have traits just to stay in the relationship.

Use your Dear God Letter as a barometer for how close you are to having the relationship of your dreams. Use it as a guide to really understand what you are looking for. If you find you're missing key elements, add to your list and keep moving forward. As we mentioned, sometimes your would like traits turn into must have traits, and sometimes you realize something that's important that wasn't on your original list at all.

Throughout your relationship, check in with yourself and ask yourself the following question: "Am I compromising any of my must have traits just to be in a relationship?" This is a critical point.

UNDERSTANDING ME, UNDERSTANDING MY RELATIONSHIP

When a relationship ends, it's a great time to take a closer look at how you engaged in the relationship. Ask yourself the following questions:

- What did you learn about you?

- Were you the person you want to be?

- What traits did you like about him?
- How did you benefit?
- What would you do differently in the next relationship as a result of what you learned?
- What did you find fulfilling about the relationship as a whole?
- Do you want to revise your Dear God Letter?

By reflecting on these questions, you can close the loop on the relationship that ends and set yourself up for success for the next relationship that's right around the corner.

Now that you have a clearer idea of what you want, it's time to evaluate the last pieces to set you up for success in your next relationship.

There are valuable lessons that we learn about ourselves following every relationship.

Use the time immediately following a relationship or even during your current relationship to make the next intimate experience with your man even better.

If your relationship lasts for a season, follow the same evaluation process.

Every relationship is important. When you look back on each relationship, be careful of your self-talk and know that it's okay if who you thought was Mr. Right turns out to be Mr. Not Right. Positive self-talk will help you get through a transition. Give yourself credit for following your heart and working toward the relationship you want. Keep moving forward on your quest for having it all.

Many times the relationships that turn out to be for a reason or a season are the relationships you learn the most from. They are the relationships that help you define what you want. They also give you an opportunity to grow as a person and move closer to understanding your authentic self.

Give yourself time to reflect and then get focused again and follow the principles. Find a way to believe again that he is out there and you do deserve him.

He'll be worth the wait!

CLOSING THE LOOP

Closing the loop on your relationship is important. Oftentimes, we want to keep the lines of communication open with the men we've dated. Recognize it was nice while it lasted. Investing time and effort in a friendship with someone you've dated pulls your attention away from giving all of you to the next romantic relationship you're seeking.

Let him go with blessings and focus on having a healthy, positive close to your relationship. Appreciate him for the time you have shared together.

Understand that falling in love and building a relationship is going to mean that you may need to work through several relationships to get clear about yourself and what you want. The faster you close your ties to the relationships and the men that are not right for you, the faster you will find the man of your dreams who wants to share the relationship you want.

POISED AND PRIMED FOR THE NEXT RELATIONSHIP

Using the Boys Before Business™ philosophy can help you find your way to the I.D.E.A.L. relationship for you.

Keep your focus on the positive and productive parts of each relationship experience. When you find a relationship isn't supportive or enjoyable, explore what's possible with the man you are dating and determine if he reflects the traits in your Dear God Letter.

If he doesn't, start again with a lot more clarity and go for the man of your dreams. Don't settle.

Be true to yourself and watch yourself grow through each relationship.

Have confidence that you will find him. Go back to the beginning of the book and start again. Have courage and faith that you are still ready to have it all. Sometimes it takes practice to really get to the right man. We know this firsthand because it took Jennifer three times to get it right. Don't give up. Just keep going.

TIPS FOR LEARNING FROM THE PAST TO BUILD THE I.D.E.A.L. RELATIONSHIP FOR YOU

Learning from the past makes it more possible for you to not repeat the same relationship. Use these tips to understand what you experienced and who you were in the relationship so you can create an even better relationship next time.

1. Write down everything that was great about the relationship. When were you most happy? What were your favorite moments?

2. Did you see any red flags that you chose to ignore?

3. Get your Dear God Letter out and evaluate how close he came to matching what you asked for. Be honest with yourself.

4. Give yourself time to go through all the emotions you have. Give yourself permission to be sad, mad or disappointed. When you're ready, get back into action and start visualizing your next relationship.

5. Use positive self-talk daily so you don't give up or fall into the trap of thinking that he's not out there.

6. Avoid going full-force into work mode. Take time for yourself and continue to do the things you love.

Keep your focus on getting Mr. Right and not settling for Mr. Good Enough.

AND... L IS FOR LUST, LOVE AND LONG TERM

Oh, the joys of a great relationship. Reveling in the excitement of holding hands or a tender kiss good night. You're ecstatic to finally feel that deep, wonderful connection with your man.

Every relationship moves through many stages. The unfolding connection you feel will deepen as you open up, share your heart with your man, and begin to celebrate the joy you feel when you know you can have everything your heart desires—your man, your business, and the life you love.

LUST: GOTTA HAVE IT

At the beginning of a relationship there are times when you'll be consumed by lust. Lust is when your heart skips a beat every time you see his name on caller ID. Lust is when you're out together and you can't wait to get home. Lust is that overwhelming feeling you never want to be apart. Lust is exciting and fun and you can feel your adrenaline racing. Embrace all these feelings and catch your breath.

You want to experience lust and cherish it. There will be higher levels of lust at the beginning because it's new and exciting—and we all want more of that! As you grow through the relationship, you'll experience different levels of lust the longer you're together. This is because, at the beginning, lust is a main focus of the relationship as you work together to determine if you're a chemistry match. Once you've established that you are, it's up to you and your man to maintain the higher levels of lust by continuing to put forth your efforts and creativity in order to capture the same feelings. This initial feeling is not always sustainable. The giddiness you feel at first may fade into a deeper sense of loving where you know it's right for you. Don't despair, love comes next. In the meantime, be grateful for this sensation when everything is new and exciting. This is part of the process.

Be creative and talk with him about what turns him on. Be sure to tell him what turns you on, too. Be true to yourself and push outside your comfort zone as far as you are willing to go. Pushing yourself too far may strain your relationship, so take good care of you and keep it fun.

When lust starts to fade, you'll still look at the phone and be excited when you see his name on caller ID. The difference will be that, instead of your heart skipping all over the place, you'll find a sense of calm and happiness and even security. Enjoy it and be excited about the next stage. Let go of the temptation to analyze this new feeling by bringing back the FOBFO™ and wondering if he's still passionate about you. Just because he doesn't call you one time doesn't mean that he's no longer in love with you. This is a normal part of the process. If you spend your time wondering why you aren't feeling giddy, you'll miss out on love…and love is better than lust.

CULTIVATING AND SUSTAINING LUST

Here are a few ideas to help you keep the passion present in your relationship and keep the fires burning when you're together and apart:

1. Create nicknames for each other that reflect how attracted you are to one another. Use terms of endearment like these and others such as honey, sweetie or baby to reinforce your desire for him.

2. Find innovative ways to keep close, physical contact when you're together, such as holding hands, putting an arm around each other, and placing a hand on each other's leg when you're sitting down. If you really want to get crazy, you can play footsy under the table and come up with other fun ways to keep each other physically stimulated.

3. Kiss in public. Make it fun. Come up with a dramatic way for him to sweep you off your feet and kiss you passionately in public. For example, you may want to have him dip you in the middle of the sidewalk just as if you were doing the tango and kiss you madly. You may both stand back up and laugh from how much fun this can be. Others will wonder how you do that and wish that they could, too. (Maybe this has been you—now it's your turn.)

4. When you greet each other at the airport or when you see each other, drop everything and leap into his arms. Free yourself of any inhibitions or limitations and fly into the arms of the man you love. He'll be pleasantly surprised, shocked, and enjoy the feeling of how free you can be with him.

5. Dance inside your house for no reason. Put your song on, grab your partner, and share a sweet moment together in each other's arms.

6. Surprise him with the unexpected. Maybe you could do a sexy, sensual striptease or cook dinner in an outfit that is not the norm for you and perhaps a bit revealing.

LOVE: NOT A SECOND-HAND EMOTION

Tina Turner sings "What's Love Got To Do With It?" We say: everything! This is when you realize you have more than just lust going for you. This is when you realize your strong affection and attraction has more to do with your shared experiences and how you interact with each other. Love is when you want to spend time with your man because being around him makes you want to be a better person and being around each other brings the best out in the both of you.

In the love stage, your confidence rises and you start to feel a sense of calm. You'll know you're in the love stage when you see that his actions and his words match consistently, you rarely FOBFO™, and you're comfortable enough to say what you are thinking or feeling. You look forward to spending time talking, going out, and just being together. The difference is now you can focus on your work without the silly distractions of wondering "what if." In fact, being in love can make your business even better. Chances are you'll bring a sense of happiness and contentment to your work. People will notice.

Even though you're in the love phase, celebrate the importance and joy of lust. Getting complacent and thinking that now that you have your man you can focus on work can weaken the bond and change your focus. Focus on work during your set work hours and always make separate time for your relationship. This strategy is what leads to long term success in both your relationship and career.

When it comes to long term, some of us know instantly that "he's the one." Others will need more time to trust their feelings and open up their hearts. If it takes you a day, a year or ten years, it's worth it.

After you have found the right partner, there are times when you're lustful and times when you're amazed about how much you can love someone else. You might even, from time to time, question whether your feelings are for real and feel like saying "pinch me" so you can believe what's happening. You might feel different when you find the long term love you have been looking for. New feelings arise that you have not experienced with any other relationship. It's common to hear yourself say, "I've never felt this way before."

When you transition into the long-term relationship, you know you're on the same page. Your vision for the future is clear together and your goals match. The most important aspect is when you are together you're 100% authentic to your core values and you always feel you can be yourself. You identify these for yourself and recognize how they match up with each other. Long term means you stay true to yourself, put your relationship first and stay true to your beliefs. You want to stay the course and keep your passion alive.

CURIOSITY CURES THE CAT

Cuddle up with your man and enjoy the passion you feel. Opening up to him feels wonderful and you may find that you want more and more of these moments. You may want to avoid feeling vulnerable or revealing your true thoughts, wants, desires and emotions. Balancing your lust, curiosity and feminine desires with the other parts of your life may seem to be a daunting task. You may prefer to appear strong, independent and self-sufficient. As hard as it is to let down your guard, the more open you are, the faster and easier your relationship will flourish.

Recognize that your relationship is a priority. Putting it first is the basic foundation of the happiness you seek. Avoiding it and taking it for granted reduces its potency and cuts the oxygen to the flames that ignited your passion in the first place. Make your relationship a top priority in your life. It will catapult your joy to a whole new level.

Just like you, your man wants your undivided attention. Give him the honor and respect of being number two in your life, after you. Focus on him and make him a priority in your day. Ask yourself: what do I want to learn about him today? What is he feeling today? If today was his last day on Earth, what would he want to do and how can I make his life more spectacular today?

BECOME A FREELANCE REPORTER

Ask, inquire, listen, and learn so you can love him deeper. Find out what makes him happy, learn what he loves, listen to his dreams, desires, and daily plans. Ask yourself: What can I do to support this amazing man in every way so he can get what he wants?

Focus on what he's telling you. Let him speak. Listen intently. Admire his strength and courage to share with you his voice, his imagination, his creativity and his essence. Find in him the actions and behaviors you love. Let him know how much you enjoy him.

If he has a moment where he's doing something that irritates you, focus on that which you love about him. Take a deep breath, think deeply about something he does that absolutely makes you laugh, turns you on or makes you feel loved. Life's irritations are fleeting and temporary. In order for them to stay and grow, we have to invite them into our lives and make them bigger than they are. A year from now, you won't remember them, so make the choice to focus on the good, strong, healthy man you have. Celebrate him by bringing out the best in him. Let him change, make new choices and grow every day. Celebrate this evolution in him.

Ask him each day: What does your day look like today? Is there anything you want me to do today for us? Is there anything I can do to support you with your day? Find out who he is and fall in love all over again. Let him grow and enthusiastically encourage him to share his humanity, his passion and his desires with you. At the end of the day, ask him how his day was and what would have made it better.

Do this for him and see how your relationship expands and evolves effortlessly. Embracing him provides him with strength and courage to reach out further faster and make a greater contribution to you and the world around you. Why would we want anything less for someone we love and adore?

TIPS FOR HOW TO CHECK IN ON YOUR RELATIONSHIP AND PASSION

As your lives get busy, take the time to check in on your relationship. Making it great can take as little as a few minutes a day. Use one or more of these tips to sustain your relationship and watch it grow.

1. Every day, ask your man on a scale of 1 – 10 how is the relationship for him. If it's not a 10, ask him what it would take to make it a 10 that day.

2. Take a few minutes each day to tell each other what you are thankful for about one another in your relationship. Appreciate your relationship and enjoy being together.

3. Check your calendar: is it filled with time set aside to spend together? Find time to make memorable moments and celebrate your relationship.

These three simple tips can keep your relationship on track and easily keep the passion alive.

ACCEPTING YOUR GREATNESS AND CELEBRATING HIS

When you look at him, see the greatness inside and out. Realize that he's all at once a little boy, a lusty teenager, a handsome prince and an amazing lover. He's someone to be celebrated and appreciated. And so are you.

Sometimes we choose to look for what's not right or how much better he could be if he just... We frustrate ourselves by wanting to change the men in our lives. This frustration unfortunately defeats the whole relationship and starves it from the very food it needs. Then this frustrated energy overflows into other areas of our lives, such as our business. Is this really what we want to have, a relationship that sinks our souls and burdens the man we so wanted to share our lives with?

Let him be who he is. Let go of those little irritations and you'll find that this love overflows into every part of your life. You'll glow with it. People around you will wonder, just like you used to, what is it that makes her shine so bright and smile like that?

By seeing his greatness in all his glory, you bring joy, encouragement, laughter, and delight to the surface of his soul. You reflect back to him the mirror of what his being in the world does for you. Give him the benefit of feeling the love, lust, and beauty that he brings into your life. Focus on the amazing relationship you have and everything that's great about it.

LIFE TREATS US THE WAY WE TREAT OURSELVES

Treat your man with the same care, compassion and joy that you want to be treated. Give him the gift of you every day. Use the golden rule: do unto him as you would want him to do unto you. Seek the beauty in him today.

Do this for yourself. Oftentimes, we tend to focus on giving our man every part of our attention and leave ourselves out. The balance and the beauty in life can be summed up in a simple statement: learn what it feels like to receive the love, admiration and adoration you want to give him by giving it to yourself first. Knowing how it feels to receive this yourself provides you with a depth of understanding so you can give this to him with deep appreciation and admiration. Love yourself and then love him. Give yourself the gifts you would give him. He'll love you for this and follow your lead. All you have to do is focus on the greatness in you, and let him reflect this back to you—in his eyes, in his actions, and in his loving embrace.

In Boys Before Business™, the joy you experience in your relationship sinks into your soul. You exude happiness and carry this feeling of being loved into your business. Customers, clients, co-workers and cohorts will wonder what you are doing differently.

When you're with him, love him, adore him, and make him the center of your attention. Leave behind the daily activities and forget about what you'll be doing in a few hours. Be with him completely. We want this same attention, so give it to him. Let him feel this from you. Let him know how good it feels for you to focus on him. Find out what turns him on, what you can do that will help him feel loved. Ask him to do this with you. Explain it to him. Help him to discover what turns you on and what makes you feel spectacular.

Neither of you can read each other's mind, so guessing or expecting that he's going to want or enjoy the same things you do is like taking a chance in a casino. Wouldn't you rather just win every time? This is what sharing this information with each other does. It takes the risk out of the activities and actions you take and takes your relationship to a whole new level.

You won't be wasting time playing games or hiding from each other. Testing his commitment isn't cultivating the relationship you seek. Instead, be transparent, be vulnerable. Let him be the same. Come together in your lives and make every connection count.

THE GOLDEN RULE

In a long-term relationship, applying the golden rule is critical to your success. Treat your mate with the love, care and compassion you desire. Spend time doing things together and appreciate the time you spend apart. *Be committed to loving him for who he is and who he wants to become, which may be different from who you want him to be.* Long-term success in a relationship is based on accepting each other for who you each are without the urge to want one of you to change.

Get involved in each other's lives and be supportive of each other's passions. Even if he loves fishing and you don't, be excited for him to go on a fishing trip. If he wants you to go and you choose to go with him, go with a good attitude and use the time to understand his passion. If you choose not to go, still encourage him to go without you. Find something to do that you are passionate about and appreciate your time apart.

There will be times when you don't agree. This is when it's even more important for you to communicate your thoughts and feelings and agree to disagree. Each of you is entitled to your opinion. Treat him as you would want to be treated in a time of conflict. Use the same communication skills you'd use in romantic times: good listening, not interrupting and articulate what's bothering you without blaming, shaming or justifying.

Long-term means you're committed to making it work. Sometimes it might require compromise. It's worth it. When you're happy in love and have the support of your long-term mate, everything else is better when you're together.

Listen to him. Love him with all your heart. Be present with him. Celebrate him. These are the ways lust turns to love, and how love breeds the long-lasting relationship you know is possible.

This synergy of boys and business is the key to having it all. Carry the love you feel each day in your relationship out into everything you do. Share it with everyone you meet. Watch as your life unfolds into one that is beyond your imagination. It's possible when you put Boys Before Business™.

REAP THE REWARDS

Now you've got it—the relationship and life of your dreams. Congratulations! The balance in life that you thought wasn't possible is now yours to enjoy, encourage and expand. The beauty of what you experience each day is beyond the imagination of your friends and family, and you feel grateful.

That's right—it's time to reap the rewards of your efforts and refreshing new Boys Before Business™ approach to your relationship.

Sustainability in relationships always seems to be a mystery. It's the elusive key that appears to be what everyone needs but no one seems to be able to figure out. To truly reap the rewards, commit to learning more about your mate every day and deepening the relationship you have cultivated.

We want you to be all you can be in every area of your life. Reaping the rewards is a celebration of how you maintain the environment, atmosphere and lifestyle you want to live. Share your biggest and best self with your man as well as everyone you touch through your business.

It's possible. Here's the secret formula:

TAKE IT TO THE LIMIT

Always work on developing the relationship so every day is better and better. Be careful about getting complacent and going back to your old habits. You've learned to develop great communication skills, set priorities and ask for what you want. Continue to practice those skills daily. With constant attention and care you can take your relationship to new heights.

The Boys Before Business™ philosophy is to work on your relationship daily so your relationship matches your Dear God Letter. By doing this, your relationship will always be in motion and keep getting better and better. As a result, you'll keep getting more of what you desire.

WORK IT

Every day is another opportunity to grow and build your relationship. What you think, feel and do changes over time and it does for your man, too. Discovering who you are and what you want from day to day helps you stay connected with your man so he can continue to support you in ways that make sense and feel good for you. You'll want to do the same for him. Why would we want anything other than the best?

The best comes from working at it. Continue to make a routine with your man to connect in your own special way in the morning, throughout the day and at night. This keeps the spark alive in your relationship and stimulates your attraction to each other.

If you want the relationship to last, cherish it. Love yourself and take good care of you and your man. A relationship that lasts is one that becomes a priority in your life. You only have twenty-four hours in a day, dedicate the time needed to properly support your connection with him. Sometimes it might be ten minutes, other times it might be an hour, and sometimes it might be the whole day. Together, determine the time you need. By making the relationship the most important part of your life after your relationship with yourself, you put your highest levels of energy, effort and action into it. This is a formula for winning and one that will sustain your relationship electricity for years.

DO IT

One way to continue to have the relationship you want is to set relationship goals. These goals can be how you want to continue feeling or how you want to spend your time together. Have clear intentions in your activities and your communication. Spend time daily reviewing what's working and what you want to improve. Be an active participant. Chances are your actions will spark more action from him.

Make plans for a great weekend, a fun night out or a great vacation. The key is to continue to do fun things together.

You also might want to have a day where he gets to pick the activities you do and where he is the center of attention. Feed his soul and do what he wants to do joyfully. Then pick a day when you get to choose what you want to do. Remember you're going to do these together so make each one a great day. This creates good balance and an appreciation for what you both love.

Together, decide what you want your life to look like. Create a dream board so you're both striving for the same goals and you have a clear vision of where you want to go.

DREAM BIG – TIPS FOR CREATING YOUR DREAM BOARD

Living the life of your dreams begins with getting clear about what this looks like. Having clear images of what is important to both of you in the relationship can be easy to visualize every day. This is the power of a dream board.

Get ready to have some fun. Creating your dream board can take a few hours or a whole day depending on how elaborate you want to be.

Here are a few ideas for how to build one and what you'll need in order to put it together:

1. Start by looking at magazines. Pick out images of those things you aspire to be, the items you want to have, words and phrases that inspire you, and other images of experiences you want to share and do together.For example, find a picture of what your dream home looks like. Identify places you want to visit on vacation. If you want to have children, are there images of families that reflect what you want to enjoy with your own? Ask yourself: do you have a dream car? Do you want to own more than one home? Is there something in particular that you want to own and enjoy?

2. Cut out each image and arrange them in a collage on the background of your choice, e.g., poster board or wood.

3. If you're electronically savvy, there are many options for you to complete this online. Check out our resources at www.BoysBeforeBusiness.com/Resources and use digital images and music to create your electronic dream board.

Put your dream board in a place where you both can see it and look at it every day. If your dream board is electronic, watch it daily and enjoy the impact it has on your growing relationship.

REFINE IT

Keep refining your relationship by redefining it. Make sure you review the environment you live and meet in. The atmosphere and culture you share with your man will become the foundation for your lifestyle and experience with each other. If your home is peaceful, clean and comfortable, then your relationship will reflect back as peaceful, clean and comfortable, too.

Atmosphere is physical and emotional. Allowing each other space and time to be together and apart is important to the overall depth of the relationship. Helping each other bring out the best in one another includes encouraging time to meditate, reflect and regroup so you can continue to share yourself and what you are learning about you.

Pay attention to your environment. This includes supporting all the rituals, routines and experiences you love to have as part of your foundation for the relationship. If you want to make love on Sunday mornings or take a walk at sunset together, then make sure that where you are is conducive to this ritual and routine. You may want to set aside a day once a week for the two of you to be together and focus on your passions. This can become a cornerstone for your relationship and a pillar of strength for your connection to grow.

VALUE IT

When you examine your relationship with each other, determine the value of the relationship and the experience you are having each day. Provide feedback for one another so you can keep raising the bar on the relationship energy you share.

The values you share in your lives that knit your beliefs together strengthen your relationship, too. Be sure to check in with each other to determine if values have shifted and if the relationship is serving the person you are becoming each day.

SHARE IT

When you're at work, bring the lessons of the relationship with your man to the business and professional relationships you're cultivating, too. It's great to feel the high energy you feel with your man in the conversations you have with business colleagues and clients. You can have both!

Use the Boys Before Business™ philosophy at work. Take the energy and experience you're building to craft and expand the relationship with your man and apply this to your business and career. Before you know it, you'll be soaring to new heights in every area of your life.

Clear focus in your relationship adds value to your work life. Use the same skills you're practicing to foster your relationship to jump start your career or give your career a boost. Learn to apply some of the same tactics. Create a dream board for your career and set career goals. Share these with your mate so he knows how to support your career dreams. As your communication grows in your personal relationship, use the same philosophy in your work place. Are you working with people who share your values and beliefs? Are you taking time to listen to co-workers, clients and vendors?

Your clients and vendors may wonder why you are glowing as your relationship with your man continues to escalate. Teach them how to have this for themselves by using the Boys Before Business™ approach in your business. Make the relationships in your business important while you're at work. When you're working, be present to those who enjoy your efforts and support your passions. When the day ends, develop a routine to celebrate the end of the day and bring closure to the work part of your day.

Then focus on your man and bring the joyful energy of your day home to share with your mate. He'll appreciate you and support you in ways you only imagined a man could.

DAILY DISCIPLINE HELPS THE DESIRE

If you want your relationship to exceed your dreams, you have to give it daily attention. Take time out for the little things. In today's world of technology you have many options to let him know you are thinking of him. A text message, email, instant message or even leaving him a note in his wallet are all great ways to show him he comes first.

Learn something new about each other daily. The more you know what excites your man and the more he understands what makes you tick, the more you will experience relationship bliss.

Celebrate your success together and find ways to share disappointment. Tell your man what will help you get through a difficult time and share with him how you want to celebrate. Understand how he deals with success and disappointments. If he wants to be alone, give him his time and freedom. Show him that you support how he deals with any situation.

Delete the word "whatever" from your vocabulary. If you have an opinion, be sure to share it. Also delete the sayings "I don't know" and "it doesn't matter." It does matter and you do know. The more you share with your mate how you feel, the more you receive what you want.

FROM WHINE TO WEALTH

As your relationship reaches new levels of communication and joy, keep acknowledging all the wonderful traits he has. Focus on what you love about him and your relationship together. Stop whining about what you don't have. Don't sweat the little things. If you care about a man who is always on time and your man is, celebrate that. Don't complain that he is always a few minutes early.

You asked for what you wanted, so be careful about changing what you want and giving him a mixed message. If you never cared what he wears and now you do, check your whine-oh-meter. Are you looking for things to complain about or has something new become important on your must have traits? Does it really matter that he wears the same thing over and over or is it more important for him being on time? If you can't decide, take action and buy him a new shirt or decide what actions you can take to benefit you both.

Chances are, there will be something about him that isn't perfect. It isn't about being perfect. It's about, is he perfect for you? Avoid focusing on his imperfections. As we've said, if you trade in one set of imperfections and go looking for someone different, what you'll find is just a different set of imperfections.

BALANCED AT LAST

The I.D.E.A.L. relationship creates balance in your life. Balance eliminates the need to complain. It encourages growth and increases your productivity. Your energy is higher and healthier so you feel you can do more.

The focus you have shifts from what could be better in your life to what's already outstanding. This gives you and your man the opportunity to experience wealth and a rich life together in many ways, including financially.

When you're enriched in your personal life, this happiness and joy is infused into your professional life. You look healthier, you feel happier and you're fun to be with. People will want to know what your secret is to having the rich life they see you leading.

MR. RIGHT CAN LEAD TO MRS. RICH

The right man will help you get rich. The kind of rich we like to talk about at Boys Before Business™ is a life that encompasses your dreams and his. Together, you become the secret ingredient for each other so you can have it all.

Mr. Right can lead right to your being Mrs. Rich. The relationship you have cultivated which is full of love and support will give you a rich life. You will have balance, vision and goals to go after. Nothing will stop you from attaining your dreams.

There is something that is freeing when you are with a man who supports your dreams and wants you to be all you can be. As an individual, his support will inspire you to do more and be more.

The best results come quickly when you're both willing to be transparent and vulnerable with each other instead of testing him to figure out if he's the one. Be yourselves. Continue to give 100% to the relationship and see how he gives 100% of himself to you.

Have the courage to be vulnerable in a relationship. It's this sweet vulnerability that becomes the catalyst to raising the intimacy of your relationship along with the trust and openness you want to feel in a safe, close, romantic bond. If you want to have the I.D.E.A.L. relationship you've always dreamed of, be willing to give all of yourself to the process of growing and feeding it. You'll reap the rewards you seek and many more beyond your imagination.

Working together as a team in life creates possibilities beyond your wildest imagination and dreams. The old adage "two heads are better than one" is absolutely true when the two heads work together and dream big together.

You'll find that you feel supported and confident in a Boys Before Business™ relationship. No more thinking about what to do about him while at work, and thinking about work when you're home with him—those days will be long gone now, a distant memory.

These days you'll be reveling in your blessed life, your dream life, and reaping the rewards every day.

This is what you've been looking for so go out and get it!

Using the Boys Before Business™ philosophy you can create the life you want. You can use the principles to find the man of your dreams and also use them to design your dream career. You can have both.

It's your time to have it all!

BBB Formula for "Having It All"

Work on yourself and know what you want.
Be prepared for the relationship of your dreams.

Make room for him in your life—clean out the clutter in your head and in your house.

Put your relationship first—that means put him before work.

Communicate and connect daily so there's no guessing or stressing about how he feels. Have conversations with him instead of in your head.

Stop FOBFO-ing and get into action.*

Be open to changing your routines.

Celebrate daily.

Passion breeds prosperity. A good relationship leads to growth in your business or workplace. It's true: you can have a great career and a great relationship.

Make the time to look great so you feel great.

Teach and train others how to treat you in your life.

Great relationships have great communication which can also improve your work life.

Be a dynamic team. You can move mountains together and grow forward as a loving couple.

Carry the feeling of being loved by your man into your business. Love your clients and customers with this same energy.

Yes! You can have it all.

* Refer to Chapter 3 for FOBFO-ing information

Join
Club BBB™

You've read the book. Now it's your turn. If you're like most people who have read about having it all, you can't wait to start putting the tips and tools into action. We're here to help you find the man of your dreams and live the life you love.

Start living the Boys Before Business™ philosophy now by joining the Club, a specially created online environment with the sole purpose to help you live and share the principles talked about in the book with other women with the same goals: a great love and a great life.

If you really want to practice what is in the book, you have to take action. Get access to our step-by-step weekly lessons which take you in-depth on how and where to find him and meet him. Each lesson covers specific information and activities to guide you on your journey.

There is no other place that offers you the support, encouragement and know-how. If you are serious about meeting him, keeping him and having a great career, then Club BBB™ is the right place for you.

Join Now.

Go to www.BoysBeforeBusiness.com/membership.html.

The Story of the Title
"Boys Before Business"

We are living proof of what you read in this book.

We believe it's possible to meet the man of your dreams, have an amazing relationship and sustain a great relationship. We also believe that when you have a great relationship, it transcends into every area of your life and your life can feed off the energy you cultivate in your relationship.

You can experience the exhilaration of being in a fantastic relationship and you can have everything you want when you put yourself and then your relationship first. We say boys before everything…Boys Before Business™.

Before we started this book, neither one of us believed we could have it all. We thought something would have to give. We had no idea that you can have it "all." That infamous "all" being for us a great love and a great career at the same time.

What changed?

We realized that we had learned so much from our past relationships in our lives and our own behaviors during them that we could craft the ultimate approach to the lives we knew we were born to live and share with someone special. We felt that having a solid intimate relationship was an important foundation for each of us to truly enjoy the fulfilling life we wanted.

When we met each other in the summer of 2007, our lives were about change—and we mean change in a big way.

We asked ourselves the big questions:

Would it be okay if we got everything we dreamed of in our lives?

If we had the tools, tips and techniques to navigate a positive, intimate, loving relationship with the men in our lives, would we go for it full out and be committed to finding and keeping the men of our dreams?

What if we could wake up each day feeling loved by the ones closest to us and feel fulfilled in every other area of our lives?

At the time, we didn't know the answers to the above questions and we didn't truly believe it was possible. Now we know it's possible. We know because it's happened to us and we know how to teach you to get the same results. You can have happily ever after.

LIFE CHANGES AND SO WILL YOU WHEN YOU PUT BOYS BEFORE BUSINESS ™

We don't know which we've had more of, jobs or boyfriends. Although it took us awhile to find a career path that made each of us happy, success in the workplace seemed to flow easily. Success in love was another story.

We never worried about our careers and were always confident that we would be successful. Kimberly stumbled into a career in advertising in the publishing world and later started her own network marketing business. Jennifer started by writing in the world of entertainment and worked through nine career transitions to find her passion as a best-selling author and sought-after book consultant. Each career has brought us great rewards. However, as our careers were growing, we were stumbling in our relationships wondering if we would ever find our own Mr. Right.

There were times when we believed that Mr. Right didn't exist. There were times when we thought we were with Mr. Right and times when we knew we weren't even with Mr. Close Enough.

We felt great about our work accomplishments but something was missing. We wanted to share our success with someone special. We wanted to have it all but we had no idea how to have it all. We knew how to be successful in our careers but we didn't know how to find the love of our lives. We didn't want to settle for just being with someone. We always believed it is better to be alone than with the wrong person.

We really wanted to believe the right man was out there for us and we wanted to experience having it all, so we got serious about focusing on finding the man of our dreams while being true to ourselves and our passions. Before we knew it, we had it all.

It all started when we met. You've heard the clichés that people come into your life for a reason and there are no coincidences—well, those statements are true for us. After a seminar, we agreed to talk daily and set goals together and be accountable to each other for our commitments.

We talked every day for 15-30 minutes and we reviewed our health, wealth and happiness goals. As days turned into months, we got to know each other's hopes and dreams. We found that both of us wanted a fulfilling relationship and were actively dating.

One night, we both had dates with men named Tom. We lived in a three-hour time difference so we agreed to text each other on how our dates went. Jennifer sent a text that said, "having a good time, he's married, it's OK."

Kimberly's response was, wow! She wanted the details. The first thing she thought was she couldn't believe this guy had the nerve to go out on a date with Jennifer and he was married. And what did she mean it's okay? Kimberly knew this was a big surprise for her, and that this was not good.

Kimberly didn't want to call Jennifer because she knew she was still out on her date, and it was now time for her to get ready for her date. The details would have to wait until the morning. Kimberly couldn't imagine how Jennifer was handling it.

Kimberly called Jennifer first thing in the morning a few minutes before their daily call. Jennifer started asking about the usual health, wealth and happiness goals. Kimberly couldn't care less about the goals, she wanted to know about the date. So, as Jennifer was talking, Kimberly interrupted and said, "Hold on, hold on...boys before business."

Little did we know that that one saying would not only turn into this book but would also become our life philosophy. We practiced what we preached, reminded each other daily of our new principle, "Boys Before Business™." We laughed, stressed, wrote our goals and laughed some more.

We wrote this book to share our experiences, and we realized that many other women were living similar lives. While we were writing the book, we discovered our purposes and passions. As we practiced the principles we were writing about, our businesses boomed and we found the loves of our lives.

Oh, and by the way, neither man is named Tom.

Conversations with the Authors Jennifer S. Wilkov & Kimberly A. Mylls

Is there some overarching message that you would like readers to take away from this book?

J: "Boys Before Business™" is a philosophy that works. Putting the man in your life first cultivates a whole new experience for many women that will charm and endear her to him in a way that she cannot imagine. Understanding your priorities and how important this fulfilling, intimate relationship is to the rest of your life experience is the reward you reap when you put "Boys Before Business™."

K: Yes, this book is about knowing who you are and what you want in a relationship. Then, when you find it, you need to cultivate your relationship and continue to work on it. It's about putting your relationship first. As cliché as this sounds, it's about putting love first and love is the most important element to life. When you are surrounded by someone you love, everything else around you works itself out. We spend too much time worrying about the little things and not enough time talking to the people we love. It also takes attention and commitment to make it work. We can't expect our relationship to be perfect all the time.

How have you applied the information you provide in this book to your own lives? How do you know it really works?

J: The life experiences we've had lend themselves to providing the reader with real life information that really works. The situations and suggestions we describe are all activities and incidences that we each lived through in our own lives. When life really works, it leaves clues about success. It's this valuable information that we felt needed to be shared with other women like us.

K: As I started this book, I started my relationship. There are tips in the book that I did to prepare myself for the man of my dreams. As we wrote each chapter and each tip, I practiced them daily with my man. There were times when I got off course but it was only minutes instead of days to get back on course. I saw friends practice these principles, and I saw their relationships improve. I saw new relationships begin and I watched my friends become happier. The philosophy works if you apply it and believe it does work. It's just like wanting to lose weight and starting a diet, you know it will work if you stick to it. The key is sticking to it and working on it every day.

Do you think it's necessary for people to talk about their relationship experiences and examine what worked well for them and what didn't? Is there danger in not taking the time to reflect on this important information?

J: Yes. By taking the time to examine the relationships that have passed, each woman has the unique opportunity to better understand herself and her choices. Perhaps there's something about that man that was fulfilling at the time and then became unimportant to her. Maybe she enjoyed a few small parts of the relationship and would want these again in the next one. Learning who you are in each relationship and how the relationship has served you and others is a great resource for creating the relationship of your dreams with the next man.

K: Communicating is the most important thing in a relationship. So many times we talk to other people about our relationship instead of the person we are in the relationship with. We often complain to the wrong person. For example, if I don't like that my lover is always late and all I do is tell my best friend how it makes me crazy, well, then, the situation doesn't get resolved. In fact, it usually gets worse. I know it's sometimes hard to articulate what is bothering you and you keep waiting for him to read your mind. I promise you: he can't read your mind. You need to take time to reflect on what you're saying to each other, what you're enjoying about the relationship, and get feedback and input. It's the only way to get more of what you want. Don't make him guess what you want——tell him. It's the easiest way for the relationship to grow.

You spend a lot of time talking about a Dear God Letter. Why is this so important?

J: Defining the relationship you want to experience is essential for your romantic success. If you can describe in detail what that relationship feels like and how you feel when you are with him, then you can let the men you meet know what you are looking for since you are clear about it yourself. A "Dear God" Letter is like a yardstick to measure the men you meet. Calling out the relationship you want gives you the knowledge and wisdom to seek only those who can fully participate in building and sharing the relationship you want to experience. It all starts with you taking the time to give God specific information about how you want to meet him and what you want to create as a result of partnering with him.

K: The Dear God Letter is a way to let the Universe know what you want. It's a way for you to really decide what you want and put it down on paper. I had my Dear God Letter in my head for years. I knew what I wanted, I just never put it in writing. Without putting it on paper, it was just a wish. It was just "sorta" out there. I said I wanted it, but I didn't believe enough in it to put it on paper. Writing the letter gives you clarity. It gives you a focal point, a vision, something to read daily and visualize daily. This is so important. This is how you can really manifest the man of your dreams. If this is your goal, then you have to write it down. Once it's written, you have an 80% chance of it coming true. If you only keep it in your head, your chances are somewhere between 3 - 6%.

You talk about "Freaking Out Before Finding Out" (FOBFO-ing) in the book. Do you think it's really possible to stop FOBFO-ing for good?

J: Yes. When the lines of communication are open in a relationship, the FOBFO-ing can stop. You can simply ask your man about his perspective on the situation and be done with it. Having faith in the relationship and being rewarded for it by his actions and words help to reduce and eliminate FOBFO-ing. It all starts and ends with you.

K: This is a great question. Even in the best relationships, it's hard not to have a moment or two when you jump to conclusions and when you have doubts. The more you pay attention to his actions and words, the less you'll find yourself FOBFO-ing. The more you communicate with your man, the faster you'll get out of a FOBFO. To stop for good, well—we are women. We want reassurance. We have the "need to know" gene, so I think we can learn to control it. Realistically, every now and then we might just slip up.

What is your sense of who your readers are and who is your ideal reader?

J: Our readers are women like us who have been through several relationships that haven't worked and want the I.D.E.A.L. relationship this time. Our ideal reader is the woman who wants to understand herself and how to choose the activities that will support her in finding and building the relationship that works. She is open to working with new information and willing to do what is needed in order to have the relationship she wants.

K: Our reader is the single woman between the ages of 35-55. She has spent many years developing a great career, had some relationships, some close and is someone who is really searching for a great relationship. She is independent and smart and really close to having it all. Maybe she has lost a little faith along the way that Prince Charming is really out there. She understands that a man is not going to "complete" her. She believes a great relationship will make her life even better.

Why did you decide to provide tips within each chapter?

J: We felt it was important to provide hands-on information about what women can do specifically to address each part of the process. We want "Boys Before Business™" to bring tools and techniques to the reader that she can easily implement as she seeks the relationship she desires. We felt this would give her the extra edge of having practical information to work with to get her to the relationship faster.

K: It is one thing to read something, it's another to live it. To get results, you have to take action. You still have to do things to prepare yourself to find him and then to stay in a great relationship. The tips are a way to get into action and remind you at the end of the chapter that you still have a little work to do to "have it all."

This book is about being the person you want to be and letting go of other people's expectations and of our own negative self-talk. The message is not new. It is simple; we have just forgotten it on our way up the corporate ladder. The message is: Love does make the world go around. With the right person, you can have it all, and you deserve to have it all.

In what ways did the experience of writing this book change your relationships and businesses?

J: Writing this book forced me to look at my own relationships and chronicle the experience I went through to get to the best romantic relationship I have enjoyed in my life. It's so much more fun to write down those activities that took time, focus and energy that in the end led to such a greater life experience.

This "magic formula" really did exist for each of us in our own individual lives. My business relationships have become much richer as a result of writing this book. I understand myself better and have the ability to relate to students and clients in a more fulfilling way. Since books are my business, I am also able to describe for them what it's like to find the ideal writing partner and how to seek their own for their books.

The Dear God Letter is one of the most powerful processes we have found in our lives. We have suggested that using this in your business as well as your romantic life can dramatically change your experience with anything that you seek. The format provides a framework to get clear about exactly what you want so you can go out and get it. And that is exactly what we did with this book.

K: I started the relationship of my dreams after writing my Dear God Letter. Chapter after chapter writing this book, I practiced what we wrote about. I learned how to be a better communicator. I learned how to ask for what I wanted and also what I needed. Every day my relationship gets better as I laugh and love more. As for my business, it has a new focus, a new energy. Instead of feeling like I have to do it all, I feel like I have a partner in life and in business.

Obviously you both have had different experiences and relationships. As co-writers, how did you so smoothly combine your ideas and information in the book?

J: We found it was easy to write about our own perspectives of each topic first. Then we simply blended our thoughts together into the text. What was so surprising and wonderful was how similar we found our individual approaches were. Oftentimes, we were able to finish each other's sentences and even wrote practically the same thing in some cases. It's rare to find such a perfect writing partner. We're truly blessed as our writing routines are effortless.

K: We both passionately believe that you can have it all. We talked about past relationships, of what we did and what we would do differently. We shared our new experiences and held each other accountable to follow the BBB philosophy. We found too that although we dated different people, we often did similar things (i.e., making up stories in our head and FOBFO-ing). We found that so many other women had the same experiences. There was a lot of "Oh my God, I did that, too," that we heard. We laughed about having similar situations. When we put them down on paper and realized how differently we chose to respond to each one, we saw a lot of ourselves and our friends in each other. This made it a lot of fun to write together.

Acknowledgments

It's a rare opportunity in life to find a book project that engages the heart, humor, and humanity of a person.

Boys Before Business emerged from living real lives during a heartfelt conversation between two friends experiencing real dates who had a true desire to build the romantic relationship of their dreams with a man.

In an amazing collaboration of focused attention and clear intention, we have enjoyed the effortless experience of bringing this book to you.

Love is the answer and joy is the journey.

A journey is more enriching when it is not taken alone.

Many others contributed to our efforts to bring this book to you, our readers.

We appreciate the following people for loving us along the way and supporting our success with *Boys Before Business*:

JENNIFER'S ACKNOWLEDGMENTS:

Writing with Kimberly Mylls has been an absolute joy and gift. I want to acknowledge Kimberly first and foremost for her amazing partnership and accountability during this project. As a first-time author, she has worked through the different stages of creating this book with great enthusiasm, eagerness and excitement. It has been a privilege to share the journey of *Boys Before Business* with Kim, from its inspiration that morning on the phone when the title popped out of our regular daily phone conversation to the book you hold in your hands before you. Thank you, Kim, for being who you are and for your loving friendship and partnership. It's an amazing experience to write, demonstrate and teach the *Boys Before Business* philosophy with you.

There are many others in my life who have contributed to my experience with this book. The events that happened in my life during the process and timing of writing and producing this book were unimaginable to many, and yet I have been recognized and acknowledged by so many for my ability to stay focused and produce this book on time for its intended release date. Thank you to everyone who has been there for me, cheering me on and celebrating the brilliance of this project with me. I appreciate each of you for your love, care, consideration, kindness and support.

Many mentors, family members and friends have contributed to my knowledge and wisdom shared in this book and my overall life experience. Whether living today or inspiring me through the lives of those who have passed on, I want to recognize the following core group of people who continue to encourage me to raise the relationships I have to their highest levels: Anthony Robbins; Jack Canfield; H.F. Ito, beloved Shintaido Sensei; Don Cardoza, beloved Aikido Sensei; Toshimitsu Ishii, beloved Shintaido Sensei; R. Buckminster Fuller; Dr. Norman Vincent Peale; Keith Cunningham; Alex Mandossian; Joel and Heidi Roberts; Helen Keller; Eleanor Roosevelt; my beautiful grandmother, Charlotte Hillsberg, and my grandparents, Philip S. Hillsberg and Fay and Al Wilkov, who have passed on in life yet still inspire me with their amazing life stories; Aunt Suzie and Uncle Dick; my parents – Marjorie Wilkov and her husband Tim Moehnke, and Howard Wilkov and his wife Betty Gottfried Wilkov; my brother Jeffrey Wilkov and his family; Manny and Vania Goldman; Tom Martin;

Joseph J. Varghese; Dr. Lin Morel; Lauren Solomon; Helen Deitelzweig; Pete Winiarski and many others.

I would also like to acknowledge the men I have met during the course of my life with whom I have built relationships—some have lasted an evening's date for dinner and others, a season in the sun. They have all facilitated much of what I have learned about me and how healthy relationships start and end. I appreciate each of them here and wish them all well in celebrating who they are in the relationship of their dreams.

Thank you to David G. Trybus, my Prince Charming, who walked into my life at potentially the worst time possible for me and who has been a dream come true. I appreciate your love for me and your great support for me, my work and the contributions I make to the Greater Good. It is a joy to walk side by side with you through this life. Thank you, Sweetheart, for sharing this amazing journey with me.

Boys Before Business was a flash of inspiration from a conversation. I acknowledge a Higher Power and God's contributions to my work and life. It is through my faith in God and humanity that I know that Prince Charming (and Princess Charming) does exist for everyone. I want to take this moment to say thank you for the divine guidance, gift, and great intuition for *Boys Before Business*.

KIMBERLY'S ACKNOWLEDGMENTS:

I wish to express my heartfelt gratitude for the people in my life who have made this book possible:

First and foremost, I want to thank my family. To my parents, Joan and Jerry, your constant encouragement, support and love have given me the belief that not only can I have it all but I deserve it all. To my sister, Shari, thank you for always being there for me. You are more than a sister—you are an amazing role model, leader, and friend. To my brother-in-law Jason, thank you for embarking on the personal growth journey with me. Your confidence in me has been a wonderful gift. To my two nephews Jacob and Kyle for bringing out the kid in me and making me realize that a little "sugar" can make a day.

Thank you to my friend Ana Ammann. You have been always been a tremendous source of support and encouragement. Thank you for always lending an ear. You are an amazing friend and I appreciate you always helping me see clearly. Your wisdom and laughter help make the journey an incredible one. A big, huge thank you for introducing me to my wonderful husband, Rob, without meeting him there would be no book.

To Jennifer Wilkov: your partnership has been one of the best experiences of my life. I appreciate your leadership, positive attitude, integrity and commitment. I could not have done this without you and more importantly I would not have wanted to. Your friendship, guidance, faith, stamina and enthusiasm have made this book possible. I have enjoyed every step in our Boys Before Business journey.

To my all of my friends: your input, advice, confidence and friendships are amazing. Being surrounded by possibility thinkers has lifted me up and helped me reach my goals. I feel blessed to have so many friends who have been there for me every step of the way.

To my Prince Charming, Rob... I can't get enough of your love. I feel a change, something moved. Thanks to you, I have the relationship I always dreamed of and it is better than I ever thought possible. Thank you for your unconditional love and belief in me and for making me laugh everyday. Thank you for reminding me to practice the principles in this book and for holding my hand on our journey together. There is no one I would rather be with.

TOGETHER:

Jennifer and Kimberly would like to acknowledge Jack Canfield and his great contributions to our lives. We met at the "Breakthrough to Success" program in the summer of 2007. *Boys Before Business*™ wouldn't be in your hands if we hadn't met that week. Thank you, Jack, for your loving friendship and life's work. We appreciate you and your support for our fabulous experience with this book.

We'd like to thank David Hancock and Rick Frishman and the entire team at Morgan James Publishing for helping us make Boys Before Business, the book, a reality.

Our deepest thanks and acknowledgment to you, the reader, for reading and integrating the philosophies of this book into your life. We appreciate your interest and support for our perspective and contributions to your journey of enjoying the healthy, fulfilling, romantic relationship in your life.

May the Boys Before Business™ philosophy bless you with the man of your dreams and may you live the life you love.

Thank you.

Boys Before Business™
Newsletter

Each Month
We share insights and information on how to enhance your I.D.E.A.L. relationship experience and put the Boys Before Business™ philosophy to work for you.

Learn
Boys Before Business™ tips and techniques so you and your relationship continue to grow. We're delighted to support you with developing your dream relationship every month of the year.

Sign Up
for the FREE Boys Before Business™ newsletter at www.BoysBeforeBusiness.com

Bonus Gift
As a bonus, you will receive instant access to our 60 minute tele-workshop that walks you step-by-step through the first steps to having it all.

Boys Before Business™ Workshops

Are you ready to put the Boys Before Business™ philosophy to the test?

Join us for a two-day workshop where you can learn more about how to attract the man of your dreams and have a great career.

You can have it all!
We'll teach you the secrets to having both.

You'll have hands-on training with Jennifer and Kimberly and you'll leave with a plan for "How To" have it all.

The workshop is designed to help you prepare for the love of your life, give you the keys to success to find him (and keep him), and to show you how to have balance so you can have a thriving business and career at the same time.

To find a workshop near you or if you want us to come to your area, email us at info@boysbeforebusiness.com or check the website, www.boysbeforebusiness.com for our upcoming events.

Speaking Engagements

Jennifer S. Wilkov and Kimberly A. Mylls are insightful, informative and inspirational speakers. Through their Boys Before Business™ approach to relationships, they enthusiastically engage audiences and reveal real-life tips, techniques and resources to turn the journey of finding the I.D.E.A.L. romantic relationship into a dream come true. Through educational, fun and interactive programs, Jennifer and Kimberly radiate passion from the platform. They encourage and inspire everyone to realize that "Yes! You can have it all!"

To have Jennifer and Kimberly bring the Boys Before Business™ experience to your next event, please e-mail info@boysbeforebusiness.com.

Affiliate Program

Now that you know the secrets to creating your Boys Before Business™ relationship…

Share the Wealth

What if you reaped the rewards while showing others how to build their I.D.E.A.L. relationship using the Boys Before Business™ philosophy?

Become an elite affiliate member of Boys Before Business™ and help us get the message out that, "'Yes! You can have it all when you put the Boys Before Business™ philosophy to work for you."

Imagine how many relationships will transform overnight when those you know learn about this great information. How many friends have given up on finding the romantic relationship of their dreams? Introduce them to this innovative new way to approach their relationships and watch love blossom again for them and many others.

It's simple, fun and easy!

Join Boys Before Business™ ~ Become an Affiliate member

Please go to www.boysbeforebusiness.com/affiliates, click on the Affiliate Program link, and fill out the form online. Raise your hand and benefit by helping others experience their I.D.E.A.L. relationship now.

We appreciate your support.

About the Authors

Jennifer S. Wilkov

Jennifer S. Wilkov has been called the quintessential writer and teacher for the 21st century. Well known for her comprehensive knowledge of the end-to-end book publishing and marketing process by students everywhere, she is an absolute encyclopedia of resources and "how-to" guidance for any activity dedicated to writing, positioning and promoting books properly in the marketplace. She is the creator of the "From Thought to Sales in 90 Days"™ Book Process and supports first-time and seasoned authors in their end-to-end book publishing and marketing endeavors through her "Your Book Is Your Hook" consulting and training programs.

As the best-selling, award winning author of the ***Dating Your Money*** series and a sought-after book consultant, Jennifer gets personal in ***Boys Before Business.*** She partners with Kimberly A. Mylls to reveal her perspective on building the dream relationship with your man.

After becoming single herself following her divorce in her mid-thirties, Jennifer went out on a lot of first dates that didn't last past dinner. The more she focused on defining the relationship she wanted, the closer she got to the man of her dreams. Here, she shares her wisdom, knowledge, and experience about what works and what doesn't with women everywhere who want to build that close, intimate relationship with a man in this fun and witty approach to putting "Boys Before Business™."

Her funny yet practical tips, tools and techniques for showing us all how to enjoy the humanity of our relationships is priceless.

Jennifer loves sharing the journey of teaching the Boys Before Business™ philosophy to women everywhere and celebrating the resulting "Prince Charming" stories with students around the world.

Kimberly A. Mylls

Kimberly Mylls is a master trainer who helps people set and achieve their goals. Following a terrific career in the advertising and publishing world, Kimberly found her true calling as an Independent Consultant and National Vice President for Arbonne International. In this well-respected position in this premiere health and wellness company, Kimberly honed her skills in the personal growth industry. She is a certified Leadership Coach and leads her growing championship team to success every year. Kimberly inspires and trains people to do what they never thought possible and live life with vision and balance.

Leaving behind Corporate America gave Kimberly the freedom and focus to build her Arbonne team and follow her passion for writing. With previous experience from writing published articles and being the Publisher of The Arizona Home Book, Kimberly fulfills her own dream of becoming a first time book author in *Boys Before Business*.

With writing partner, Jennifer S. Wilkov, Kimberly happily shares her journey from being single to finding the man of her dreams and having it all. Upon turning 40 and never having been married, Kimberly always believed she would find "Mr. Right" – and, sure enough, she did. She met her Prince Charming, got engaged and married all within nine months. In *Boys Before Business*, she shares how she found her ideal man, how she maintains an incredible relationship, and how she is able to grow a successful business.

Kimberly did it: she transformed from the single girl looking for love to the married woman who now has it all. As part of the process Kimberly co-founded The Dear God Project to teach people how to take the first step in living their best life. She developed www.DearGodLetter.com to provide people with the same tool she used to find her true love and grow her business.

She is passionate about sharing her story through teaching the Boys Before Business™ philosophy to women everywhere so they can achieve their own happily ever after.

BUY A SHARE OF THE FUTURE IN YOUR COMMUNITY

These certificates make great holiday, graduation and birthday gifts that can be personalized with the recipient's name. The cost of one S.H.A.R.E. or one square foot is $54.17. The personalized certificate is suitable for framing and will state the number of shares purchased and the amount of each share, as well as the recipient's name. The home that you participate in "building" will last for many years and will continue to grow in value.

Here is a sample SHARE certificate:

THIS CERTIFIES THAT

YOUR NAME HERE

HAS INVESTED IN A HOME FOR A DESERVING FAMILY

1985-2005

TWENTY YEARS OF BUILDING FUTURES IN OUR
COMMUNITY ONE HOME AT A TIME

1200 SQUARE FOOT HOUSE @ $65,000 = $54.17 PER SQUARE FOOT
This certificate represents a tax-deductible donation. It has no cash value.

YES, I WOULD LIKE TO HELP!

I support the work that Habitat for Humanity does and I want to be part of the excitement! As a donor, I will receive periodic updates on your construction activities but, more importantly, I know my gift will help a family in our community realize the dream of homeownership. **I would like to SHARE in your efforts against substandard housing in my community!** *(Please print below)*

PLEASE SEND ME _____ SHARES at $54.17 EACH = $ $_____

In Honor Of: _____

Occasion: (Circle One)   HOLIDAY   BIRTHDAY   ANNIVERSARY

       OTHER: _____

Address of Recipient: _____

Gift From: _____   *Donor Address:* _____

Donor Email: _____

I AM ENCLOSING A CHECK FOR $ $_____ **PAYABLE TO HABITAT FOR HUMANITY OR** PLEASE CHARGE MY VISA OR MASTERCARD *(CIRCLE ONE)*

Card Number _____ Expiration Date: _____

Name as it appears on Credit Card _____ Charge Amount $ _____

Signature _____

Billing Address _____

Telephone # Day _____ Eve _____

PLEASE NOTE: Your contribution is tax-deductible to the fullest extent allowed by law.
Habitat for Humanity • P.O. Box 1443 • Newport News, VA 23601 • 757-596-5553
www.HelpHabitatforHumanity.org